a Taste *of*

transcendence

a Taste of transcendence

Swami B.B. Tirtha Maharaj

MANDALA
PUBLISHING

San Rafael

Mandala Publishing Group

2240-B 4th Street
San Rafael, CA 94901
telephone. 415.460.6112
fax. 415.460.5218
orders. 800.688.2218
web site. www.mandala.org
e-mail. mandala@mandala.org

ISBN: 1-886069-71-9

Printed in China
through Palace Press International

Table *of* CONTENTS

Śrīla Bhaktisiddhānta Sarasvatī Thākura

Śrīla Bhakti Dayita Mādhava Gosvāmī Mahārāja

ŚRĪLA BHAKTI BALLABH TĪRTHA GOSVĀMĪ MAHĀRĀJA

foreword

by

GOKUL
GLOBAL ORGANIZATION
OF
KRISHNACHAITANYA'S
UNIVERSAL LOVE

The author of this publication, His Holiness Śrīla Bhakti Ballabh Tīrtha Gosvāmī Mahārāja, is often heard to say, "If we hear about temporary, material topics, then we shall think temporary, material thoughts. If, however, we hear about eternal, transcendental topics, then we shall think eternal, transcendental thoughts." It follows, then, that if we have the desire to utilize our intelligence for its actual purpose—to transcend the fetters of mundane materi-al existence and its concomitant miseries and, much more importantly, to establish, through devotion, our relationship with the Lord of our heart, Śrī Kṛṣṇa—then we should hear *hari-kathā*, discussions of the transcendental activities of the Lord and His intimate associates, whenever and wherever possible. By lending our ears to these ever fresh and infinitely expanding relishable topics, our minds will be irresistibly drawn toward that ultimately attractive Supreme Personality, Śrī Kṛṣṇa.

All the sacred scriptures tell us that association begins with hearing. Yet, in order to receive its fullest benefit, that which we hear must emanate from the Lotus Lips of a *śuddha bhakta*, a person who is transcendentally situated and has exclusive one-pointed devotion to the Supreme Lord. The heart of such a rare, saintly person, who bathes in the infinite ocean of *kṛṣṇa-prema*, is always saturated with *bhakti*. When one holds cold ice close to the body, one becomes cold. When one holds a hot flame close to the body, one becomes hot. When one holds the devotionally surcharged words of a *śuddha bhakta* close to the heart, one becomes a devotee. In other words, to attain *śreyaḥ*, our eternal welfare, we must associate with and hear from a pure devotee, for it is only from such a person that we can obtain devotion. His Holiness Śrīla Bhakti Ballabh Tīrtha Gosvāmī Mahārāja is widely recognized as such a *śuddha bhakta*.

In recent years, Śrīla Tīrtha Mahārāja, despite his many duties as President/*Ācārya* of Śrī Caitanya Gauḍīya Maṭha, has traveled extensively throughout the world, gracing all with his divine realizations and inspiring many to take up the devotional path. His dynamic speeches are notable for their degree of sincerity and depth of understanding. His personal traits of affection, humility and surrender to his most beloved Gurudeva, His Holiness Nityalīlāpraviṣṭa Oṁ Viṣṇupāda Śrīla Bhakti Dayita Mādhava Gosvāmī Mahārāja, are ever-present. It is difficult to imagine any heart that would not be moved by his warm words of wisdom. This present book is a humble attempt to present the eternal, transcendental thoughts of a *śuddha bhakta* in the form of a collection of English discourses delivered by Śrīla Tīrtha Mahārāja between 1997 and 2000 in the US, Europe and India. It is hoped that these sublime lectures will provide the readers with new perspectives on the science of *bhakti*, encouragement in their *sādhana* and, ultimately, a taste of transcendence.

The editors humbly beg the readers' forgiveness for any errors or omissions that may have inadvertently crept into this publication.

Maṅgalācaraṇa

sākṣād-dharitvena samasta śāstrair
uktas tathā bhāvyata eva sadbhiḥ
kintu prabhor yah priya eva tasya
vande guroḥ śrī-caraṇāravindam

"The spiritual master is to be honored as much as the Supreme Lord because he is the most confidential servitor of the Lord. This is acknowledged in all revealed scriptures and followed by all authorities. I offer my respectful obeisances unto the lotus feet of such a spiritual master, who is a bonafide representative of Śrī Hari."

vāñchā-kalpatarubhyaś ca
kṛpā-sindhubhya eva ca
patitānāṁ pāvanebhyo
vaiṣṇavebhyo namo namaḥ

"I am repeatedly making obeisances to the *vaiṣṇavas* who fulfill all desires like a wish-yielding tree, who are an ocean of graciousness to all and who are redeemers of the fallen souls."

saṅkarṣaṇaḥ kāraṇa-toya-śāyī
garbhoda-śāyī ca payobdhi-śāyī
śeṣaś ca yasyāṁśa-kalāḥ sa ṅityā-
nandākhya-rāmaḥ śaraṇaṁ mamāstu

"I take absolute shelter of Śrīman Nityānanda Prabhu, Who is Baladeva Himself and Whose partial manifestations and parts of the partial manifestations are Saṅkarṣaṇa, Karanabdhiśāyī, Garbhodaśāyī, Kṣīrodaśāyī and Śeṣa."

Kāraṇatoyaśāyī (or Kāraṇabdhiśāyī): The first *Puruṣāvatāra*. He is the first manifestation of the Supreme Being with respect to the creation of infinite *brahmāṇḍas* (universes). He lies on the Causal Ocean.

Garbhodaśāyī: The second *Puruṣāvatāra*. He is the second manifestation of the Supreme Being lying on the ocean produced by His sweat. He is the Indwelling Oversoul and Sustainer of the infinite *brahmāṇḍas* created by the first *Puruṣāvatāra*.

Payobdhiśāyī (or Kṣīrodakaśāyī): The third *Puruṣāvatāra*. He is the third manifestation of the Supreme Being, lying on the Milk Ocean, Whom the demigods approach to be rescued from the oppression of the demons. He is the Indwelling Monitor and Sustainer of each *brahmāṇḍa* and every spirit soul.

Śeṣa: the last manifestation of the Supreme Being Who, in the form of a huge serpent, holds all the worlds on His head as if they were no heavier than mustard seeds.

namo mahā-vadānyāya
kṛṣṇa-prema-pradāya te
kṛṣṇāya kṛṣṇa-caitanya
nāmne gaura-tviṣe namaḥ

"I pay my innumerable prostrated obeisances to the Lotus Feet of the Supreme Lord, Who is Kṛṣṇa Himself, Whose Name is Kṛṣṇa-caitanya, Whose complexion is golden, Who is most munificent and Who is the bestower of *kṛṣṇa-prema* (love for Kṛṣṇa)."

tapta-kāñcana-gaurāṅgi
rādhe vṛndāvaneśvari
vṛṣabhānu-sute devi
praṇamāmi hari-priye

"O Goddess, Śrī Radhe! O daughter of Śrī Vṛṣabhānu! You are the beloved consort of Śrī Hari. Your complexion is like molten gold and You are the presiding deity of Vṛndāvana. I pay my innumerable prostrated obeisances to Your Lotus Feet."

he kṛṣṇa karunā-sindho
dīna-bandho jagat-pate
gopeśa gopikā-kānta
rādhā-kānta namo 'stu te

"O Supreme Lord Śrī Kṛṣṇa, You are an ocean of kindness. You are the friend of the submissive, Lord of the world, Lord of the *gopās* (cowherd men of Vṛndāvana), beloved consort of the *gopīs* (cowherd ladies of Vṛndāvana) and the most beloved consort of Rādhā. I pay my innumerable prostrated obeisances to Your Lotus Feet."

vande nandavraja-strīnāṁ
pādare numabhīkṣṇaśaḥ
yāsāṁ harikathodgītāṁ
punāti bhubanatrayam

"I always sing in adoration the glories of the dust of the Lotus Feet of the *gopīs* of Nanda-Vraja-Dhāma (the transcendental realm of the sweet pastimes of Nandanandana Śrī Kṛṣṇa), Whose *kṛṣṇa-kathā* (narration of the glories of the Name, Form, Attributes, Entourage and Pastimes of Lord Kṛṣṇa) sanctifies the three worlds (heaven, earth and the underworld)—the entire universe."

bhaktyā vihīna aparādhalakṣaiḥ
kṣiptāśca kāmādi tarangamadhye
kṛpāmayi tvāṁ śaranaṁ prapannā
vṛnde numaste caranāravindam

"I am devoid of devotion, replete with millions of offenses and distracted by waves of evil desires. O compassionate Vṛndā-devī, I take shelter of You and pay my innumerable prostrated obeisances to Your Lotus Feet. Kindly rescue me."

śrī-kṛṣṇa-caitanya
prabhu-nityānanda
śrī-advaita-gadādhara
śrīvāsādi-gaura-bhakta-vṛnda

"I offer my obeisances to Śrī Kṛṣṇacaitanya, Prabhu Nityānanda, Śrī Advaita, Gadādhara, Śrīvāsa and all others in the line of devotion."

hare kṛṣṇa hare kṛṣṇa
kṛṣṇa kṛṣṇa hare hare
hare rāma hare rāma
rāma rāma hare hare

First of all, I pay my innumerable prostrated, humble obeisances to the Lotus Feet of my most revered Gurudeva, Om Viṣṇupāda 108 Śrī Śrīmad Bhakti Dayita Mādhava Gosvāmī Mahārāja, and pray for His causeless mercy to give me strength, to sing the glories of Supreme Lord Śrī Kṛṣṇa, to purify my mind and to get one-pointed, exclusive devotion to Śrī Kṛṣṇa. I also pay my innumerable, prostrated, humble obeisances to the Lotus Feet of my *śikṣā* gurus and pray for their causeless mercy, to give me strength, to sing the glories of Supreme Lord Śrī Kṛṣṇa, to purify my mind and to get exclusive devotion to Śrī Kṛṣṇa. I pay my due respects to all who are present here.

The Welfare of the Living Being

There are two paths. Adopting the path that leads to your eternal welfare is known as *śreyaḥ* and adopting the path by which you can obtain pleasure of the senses is known as *preyaḥ*. Although something may be pleasing to the material senses, the consequences will be detrimental. If, however, you take to the path of *śreyaḥ*, at first it will be like poison because you have to restrict and withdraw your senses. You have to be regulated. You cannot do whatever you like. It seems like poison at first, but the fruit, the ultimate result, is ambrosia. This is not worldly ambrosia, but the ambrosia of eternal welfare. You can obtain the Supreme Lord, Who is All-bliss. If you adopt the path of pleasure of the senses, it will seem like ambrosia at first, but the consequences will be like poison—venomous poison. Therefore, which path should you take?

Ninety-nine percent of all people are running after sensuous, apparent enjoyment. They are not thinking about the consequences. They cannot perform worship of God. But those who take to the path of *śreyaḥ*, those who perform penance, austerity and the like, withdraw the senses from the objects of the senses and worship God. At first it may seem like poison because you are restricted from searching for pleasure and from doing whatever you like, according to your own sweet will. No! This sort of activity is spoiled, but if you can tolerate this, ultimately you will obtain eternal bliss. The candidates for this will be very few. As previously stated, ninety-nine percent of all people are running after sensuous, apparent pleasure. There may be one person, only one person, out of a thousand people who is interested in the path of *śreyaḥ*.

Now, in this age, we have to take a vote between *śreyaḥ* and *preyaḥ mārga*, the path of obtaining one's eternal welfare and the path of obtaining apparent pleasures. If you want the vote of the general masses, then you will be defeated by advocating the path of *śreyaḥ*. Perhaps ten or twelve persons will vote for *śreyaḥ* but several *crores* (tens of millions) will vote against it. If this were to be decided by the popular vote of the masses, then the *preyaḥ* path, that which is pleasing, would win.

It is said in *Kaṭhopaniṣad*:

śreyaś ca preyaś ca manuṣyam etas
tau samparītya vivinakti dhīrāḥ
śreyo hi dhīro 'bhipreyaso vṛṇīte
preyo mando yogakṣemān vṛṇīte
(*Kaṭhopaniṣad* 2.2)

Kaṭhopaniṣad says there are two paths. One is the path for gaining one's eternal welfare and the other is the path for obtaining the apparent pleasures of the senses. Human beings may be divided into two categories. There are persons who adopt the path of eternal welfare, and there are persons who adopt the path of obtaining apparent sense pleasure. But those who are wise, who have depth of heart, know that if you adopt the path of pleasure, you will become entangled in this world of temporary things. You will be in bondage. If, however, you adopt the *śreyaḥ* path, then you will get absolute bliss. Who can understand this? Only a wise person can—one who is actually wise, not so-called wise. Such as person can differentiate between *śreyaḥ* and *preyaḥ*. Thus, he gives up the path of pleasure and adopts the path of eternal welfare.

The path of pleasure is called "*yogakṣema*." This means that you give your full energy to gain objects of enjoyment, so that you can experience sense gratification. In this way, all of your energy is spent in the pursuit of the acquisition of money and objects of enjoyment.

After attaining all these things, you attempt to retain them. After earning money, all of your energy is spent in trying to preserve it. Those who have chosen the path of sense gratification are behaving like this. Our Param Pūjyapāda Śrīla A. C. Bhaktivedanta Svāmī Mahārāja calls such a person "fool number one."

Another verse tells us what we should do for our eternal welfare:

labdhvā su-durlabham idaṁ bahu-sambhavānte
mānuṣyam artha-dam anityam apīha dhīraḥ
tūrṇaṁ yateta na pated anu-mṛtyu yāvan
niḥśreyasāya viṣayaḥ khalu sarvataḥ syāt
(Śrīmad Bhāgavatam, 11.9.29)

This verse from *Śrīmad Bhāgavatam* is the statement of an anchorite, an *avadhūta*. Here, Śrī Kṛṣṇa is relating to Uddhava the story of an *avadhūta* who once gave advice to Mahārāja Yadu. This human birth is extremely difficult to get. *Durlabham* means "difficult to get." *Su-durlabham* means "extremely difficult to get"—almost unobtainable. One may get this precious human birth, which is very difficult to obtain, after numerous births (*bahu-sambhavānte*). Specifically, we come to this human birth after 80 lakhs (8,000,000) of births in various species. In the scriptures, it is said:

jalajā nava-lakṣāṇi
sthāvarā lakṣa-viṁśati
kṛmayo rudra-saṅkhyakāḥ
pakṣiṇāṁ daśa-lakṣaṇam
triṁśal-lakṣāṇi paśavaḥ
catur-lakṣāṇi mānuṣāḥ
(Padma Purāṇa)

You must take birth as an aquatic animal: fish, crocodile, shark, whale, etc. How many times? Nine lakhs (900,000). Those who eat a fish will be killed as a fish two times. You will find many people catching fish and killing them. We also, at some time, have been caught and devoured by them. So much suffering is there! Big fish in the sea eat the smaller fish for their sustenance. Small fish are the life of big fish. We call this "survival of the fittest." But even the big fish are not safe in the sea. In this way, we pass through nine lakhs of life of aquatic animals. Do we think about this? As fish, we experience extreme, unbearable suffering.

We are also born as trees, mountains and hills. One may argue, "A hill is inert. How can a living being become lifeless?" Actually, a hill is not inert. It grows, but it has an enveloped consciousness. Trees also have some feeling of sensation. They have life in them. Twenty lakhs (2,000,000) of births we pass this way. So much suffering! Think about this. Don't take it lightly. Look now at all the living beings in this world, who are born as trees, mountains, etc. All the other living beings are busy enjoying them. When one living being enjoys another living being, the reaction is that he takes birth as a tree, mountain, etc. As trees and mountains, everyone will enjoy us and we will be forced to remain in one place tolerating this.

There are so many worms that live in feces and the stool of animals. We will take birth as such worms for 11 lakhs (1,100,000) of births. After that, we will take 10 lakhs (1,000,000) of births in various species of birds. Some of these birds are food for humans. Chopping up our bodies, they eat us. Tremendous suffering! After that, there are 30 lakhs of births (3,000,000) as beasts such as dogs, cats, goats, etc.

Having passed through these 80 lakhs (8,000,000) of births, we have only 4 lakhs (400,000) of births remaining, which comprise the different human species. We have now obtained this precious, extremely difficult to obtain, human birth. What then should we do?

Mānuṣyam artha-dam: *Artha* means requirement, necessity. What is it we require? Unless we get absolute bliss, we cannot be happy. We may obtain other, small objects that satisfy our immediate needs. But you can get absolute bliss by getting Whom, you get all and by knowing Whom, you know all. *Artha-dam* means we can get God, the Supreme Lord, Complete Reality. But, *anityam*: at any moment we may lose this chance. We say that we shall do it in the next birth, but there is no guarantee that in the next birth we will be born as a human being. If, at the time of death, you think about some non-eternal things of this material world, you will obtain a body in an appropriate species in your next birth.

You will find evidence of this in the 5th Canto of *Śrīmad Bhāgavatam* in the story of Mahārāja Bharata, the eldest son of Ṛṣabhadeva, in which he became a deer. But we have personally seen an instance of this in our Maṭha in Gowalpada, Assam. At that time, many years ago, it was a very beautiful jungle-like area with forests, hills and rivers. All kinds of beasts lived in that area, including tigers and monkeys. The population was comprised of both Hindus and Muslims, the wealthy people coming mainly from the Muslim community. There were generally no quarrels between Hindus and Muslims and they lived peacefully side-by-side. They had love for each other. One Hindu man had to arrange for the marriage of his daughter, but was in need of money for this. No Hindu could possibly lend him so much money, so he went to a wealthy Muslim for help. In that small town, everyone knew everyone else.

"Why have you come?" the Muslim man asked.

"I have come to borrow some money," the Hindu man explained. "I have to arrange for my daughter's wedding and I have no money for this. I will pay it back."

"How much do you require?" the Muslim asked and the Hindu told him. The Muslim knew that the Hindu would never be able to pay him back, as he was very poor. With no expectation of repayment, he said, "Your daughter will be married! Here, I shall give you the money. You are my neighbor."

The marriage took place and no one in the village knew where the Hindu man had gotten the money. After fifteen years, the Hindu man died. The Hindu man also had a son, who, by God's grace, managed to become a well-to-do person. One night, the man's son had a dream. In the dream, his father came to him and said, "You do not know the circumstances of your sister's marriage. I borrowed money from the Muslim (whom he mentioned by name) but I was unable to pay him back, even though I gave my word. Because of this, I was born as a dog in the Muslim's house. You must pay back the money (he told him the amount) and I shall be delivered from this birth."

The son woke from the dream and was astonished. He thought, "My father never said anything about going to that person for money." The Muslim was renowned throughout the village. He went to the Muslim's house and inquired, "Perhaps, my father at some time borrowed something from you?"

"Go, go, go!" the Muslim protested. "You should not think about this!"

"What was the amount?" the son asked.

"Why are you worried about this?" the Muslim asked. But after some persuasion, he told the son what the amount was.

Then the son asked, "Is there a dog in your house?"

"Yes," the Muslim answered. "How do you know this?"

"May I see him?" the son asked.

The Muslim called the dog out to them. The dog, seeing his son in human form, started to weep. The son then said, "You must take this money!"

He gave back the money to the Muslim, and the dog promptly died.

This is fact. It is not just a story.

We must remember that, after this life, there is no guarantee that we shall get a human birth again. *Tūrṇaṁ yateta*: we should start *bhajana* immediately! *Anu-mṛtyu yāvan*: we must do this before death—as long as the body is fit. *Niḥśreyasāya*: for one's own eternal welfare. Try to get that eternal welfare. Eternal bliss is the Supreme Lord, so you should engage yourself in the service of the Supreme Lord. You should worship Him. Only in this human birth can you do this. You can get the objects of enjoyment in any birth, wherever you may go. As long as the elements of earth, water, fire, air and ether are there, then the qualities of those elements will also be there. You will derive sense gratification from them. The ears will be able to enjoy beautiful, sweet sounds. In every birth, you will find sense pleasures, but you will not be able to worship. So, we should perform worship—immediately!

This verse (11.9.29) was explained by our Paramgurudeva, Śrīla Bhaktisiddhānta Sarasvatī Thākura, continuously for one month, and still he said that the explanation was incomplete. In spite of his explaining it for one month, he was not satisfied because this is transcendental sound, not material sound. If you want to perform *bhajana*, then you have to understand this. If you cannot differentiate between transcendental sound and material sound, you cannot make progress in spiritual life.

In our Maṭha, you will find that, every day, the devotees repeat the same thing. Every morning and every evening is *āratika* and *kīrtana*. Is there anything new? They've already heard all this! But, our Gurumahārāja and our Paramgurumahārāja instructed us that we must repeatedly hear these things, daily. There is *āratika* in the morning, *āratika* at midday and *āratika* in the evening—the same program every day. We hear the glorification of the Vaiṣṇavas, the glories of the Guru—all is the same every day. Even *kṛṣṇa-nāma* is the same.

Nārada Gosvāmī has been uttering *kṛṣṇa-nāma* from time immemorial. But still, he cannot completely taste *kṛṣṇa-nāma*. When speaking of the glories of the utterance of the names of Śrī Śrī Rādhā-Kṛṣṇa, Caitanya Mahāprabhu said, "*prati-padaṁ pūrṇāmṛtāsvā-*

danaṁ." At every step, you experience the taste of full, complete, transcendental ambrosia. It will never become stale. God is transcendental and the worshipper of God is also transcendental. God is infinite and the worshipper of God, the Vaiṣṇava, is also infinite. Their qualities are infinite. If you say, "I have finished it—it has become stale! Find something new for me," then you have not understood anything. Caitanya Mahāprabhu did not hear about the lives of Dhruva and Prahlāda once only. "We have not yet heard the full story," He would say. We might say that we have heard the biographies of Dhruva and Prahlāda, but Caitanya Mahāprabhu wished to hear the full biographies not one time, but one hundred times. "Again!" He would say, "Please tell Me again." If, after hearing, you have the desire to hear again, then you have entered into the spiritual, devotional realm. Otherwise, you are outside and have learned nothing about spiritual life—nothing.

When our Maṭha was on Rashbihari Avenue in Calcutta, there was a person who used to attend regularly to hear religious discourses, even in inclement weather. Other persons might not show up, but he would always come. We would praise him, "You have a good taste for spiritual things." After hearing discourses continuously for eight or nine months, that person suddenly stopped coming to the Maṭha. We asked some of the other people who attended the discourses, "Where is he? What is the matter?" They said, "We have seen him, but we do not know his address." We thought that perhaps he had left Calcutta, or perhaps he was ill or otherwise indisposed. We had no way to contact him. But, one day, by the Lord's desire, while I was going through the streets of Calcutta, I met him.

"Oh," I said, "We have been deprived of your company for a long time. Were you not here in Calcutta?"

"No," he said, "I have always been here."

"Then, why have you not been coming? Have you been ill?"

"No," he said. "I have been to your place. I have heard everything.

Your only advice is 'worship Kṛṣṇa, worship Kṛṣṇa, perform *harināma*'. If there is some new thing, then I shall come again. I've already heard it all."

So, there is no new thing. You have to do *harināma*. This person attended the meetings for intellectual stimulation, not for *bhajana*. If he had come to the temple with the desire to perform worship, then God's grace would have come to him and at every step he would have found a new taste of ambrosia—a taste of the transcendental. No aspect of transcendental things can become stale. *Prasādam* cannot become stale. The glories of the transcendental cannot become stale. Nothing of this can become stale. Perhaps, upon hearing about Vraja-maṇḍala, the place of twelve *vanas* (forests), you say, "I have already heard about the twelve *vanas* several times. It has become stale. Let me hear about another, new *vana*!" No! No! Then, you have not heard anything. If you can get merely a glimpse of just one of these *vanas*, your whole life will be changed and you will be rescued from rebirth. It is written in *Caitanya Caritāmṛta* that Kṛṣṇa possesses infinite qualities and sixty-four of these are His principal qualities. If you get even a glimpse of just one of these transcendental qualities, then your life will be successful and you will be rescued. All your afflictions and miseries will be destroyed. But, we are uttering the sixty-four qualities, and we are still experiencing these miseries. This means that these transcendental qualities are not descending into us. We have not touched them, even though we may think that we have. "*Phalena phala-kāraṇam anumīyate*" (from the doctrines of *Nyāya*, or logic). By the fruit, we can understand whether or not we have come in contact with Kṛṣṇa. You may perform worship daily, but you cannot say, "I have worshipped for two years. Now I am giving it up to do other things." When you perform any kind of *bhajana*, if it comes from the core of the heart, you will never be able to give up the worship of your most beloved. When you get a spontaneous glimpse of contact with Kṛṣṇa, you will experience a thrilling sensation of ecstasy. How could you give that up? You will not wish to give up any form of devotion. When there is the thought in your mind to give up worship, then it means that you have not come in contact with Bhagavān and the transcendental qualities of Bhagavān. Only outside, externally, by intellect and mental capacity are you trying to imagine Bhagavān. Worship cannot be given up. You must repeat the same thing again and again.

Today I have explained this verse from *Śrīmad Bhāgavatam*. Suppose tomorrow I speak on it again, and then again the next day. By the third day, some listeners may say, "Oh, this is the same verse. Why don't you say something new?" We would say in reply, "Our Bhaktisiddhānta Sarasvatī Ṭhākura explained this verse for one month and still he was not satisfied. But, after hearing this verse for only three days it has become stale to you! What are you hearing?" When Śrīla Bhaktisiddhānta Sarasvatī was explaining this verse at the Maṭha at Number One Ultadanga Road, some college students had heard that a very great personality, a saint, who had a glowing, golden complexion, had come. They went to hear him speak and were astonished, as they had never seen such a powerful person before. Again, Śrīla Bhaktisiddhānta Sarasvatī was explaining that *śloka*. "*Tūrṇaṁ yateta*," he said, "Immediately start *bhajana*! Without losing a moment!"

The students consulted one another. "What is this?" they asked each other. "He is looking at us. He is directing us."

"You will not allow us to return to our homes?" the students asked.

"No!" replied Śrīla Bhaktisiddhānta Sarasvatī.

"Oh," the students thought. "It was a great mistake coming here."

Śrīla Bhaktisiddhānta Sarasvatī continued, "By traveling on the road, you may die! Start *bhajana,* right now, immediately!"

The students asked each other, "What can we do?"

Śrīla Bhaktisiddhānta Sarasvatī continued, "If your house is on fire, do you try to extinguish it or do you let everything be destroyed?"

One of the students said, "If I do not extinguish the fire at my own house, then all the other houses will also be destroyed."

"Let all the houses of the world be destroyed! Are you from this world?

brahma-bhutaḥ prasannātmā
na śocati na kāṅkṣati
samaḥ sarveṣu bhūteṣu
mad-bhaktiṁ labhate parām
(Bhagavad-gītā, 18.54)

You have come from Brahman. If someone flies in the sky, and there is an earthquake, what will he feel? If you remain in this world, then the up and down afflictions of this world will cause you to suffer and disturb your mind. But if you transcend it, then where will these afflictions be? You do not come from matter. You come from Brahman. You are thinking that you have come from matter but, in actuality, you have no connection with this matter. Immediately, from this moment on, start *bhajana*!"

The students could not leave. They were trapped. Such was the students' first lesson given by that great personality, Śrīla Bhaktisiddhānta Sarasvatī Gosvāmī. The students were so attracted by his personality, that they did not return to their homes. With their books, they remained there. Do we have such power to persuade someone to stay? He had such spiritual attraction and power. Within a very short time, he preached the doctrine of divine love throughout the world.

Nothing spiritual is stale. Our organs of the material senses are stale. We do not feel our spiritual senses. They have not yet manifested themselves. By means of material senses, you are trying to understand the words of a *śuddha bhakta*. You are trying to get the sweetness of the Deity by means of material senses. It cannot be done. These things are not material, they are spiritual.

nāma vigraha svarūpa—tina eka-rūpa
tine 'bheda' nahi—tine 'cid-ānanda-rūpa'
(Caitanya Caritāmṛta, Madhya-līlā, 17.131)

Name, Deity and the Form of Kṛṣṇa are all *saccidānanda*. But we do not understand this. What can be done?

What is Bhakti?

We have all traveled to many holy places in Vraja-maṇḍala, participating in many religious festivals. Presently, we are participating in Jhulan-Yātrā, the "Swing Festival," of Rādhā-Kṛṣṇa in Vṛndāvana. Actually, it was performed in Kāmyavana from Ekādaśī to Pūrṇimā, the full moon. We generally perform *vaidhī-bhakti—bhakti* as per the injunctions of the scriptures. We are not entitled to perform *rāga-bhakti*. We are not in that position. Our *guru-varga* has introduced this practice as *vaidhī-bhakti*. But, what is the actual definition of *bhakti*? We are busy moving from one place to another. We have circumambulated Gīrīrāja and Vraja-maṇḍala with the Vaiṣṇavas. We perform this kind of devotional activity, going to the various holy places of pilgrimage. We go to these places to participate in the holy festivals and to hear about the Supreme Lord's Names, Forms, Attributes, etc., from a *śuddha bhakta*—a pure devotee. We chant, we remember. We are engaged in all these devotional forms but, at the same time, we remain attached to worldly objects. We do not experience any improvement. What is the cause?

If you do not understand the definition of *bhakti*, then, throughout your life, even though you continue to perform *bhajana*, you will derive no actual benefit.

sarvopādhi vinir-muktaṁ
tat-paratvena nirmalam
(Bhakti-Rasāmṛta-Sindhu, Purva Vibhāga, 1.10)

What is *upādhi*? *Upādhi* is any quality that you have acquired by performing some action. "Now, I have become a professor." I am not a professor, but I have gone through the education process and, having become employed, I am now called "professor." I am not actually a professor. I am not actually a doctor, etc. These are all qualities I have obtained. This is known as "*upādhi*": title. They are denotations by which one individual is distinguished from another. All such denotations are there. But, with these false egos, misconceptions, we cannot perform *bhakti*. We think that we belong to the designations of *varṇāśrama-dharma*: *brāhmaṇa, kṣatriya, vaiśya, śūdra, sannyāsī, vānaprastha, gṛhastha, brahmacārī*. We think, "I am of India, I am of Uttar Pradesh, I am of Delhi, I am of Punjab, I am of London. All these false egos have to be given up completely. Not even one cent of them should remain. "*Sarvopādhi vinir-muktaṁ*": we have to remove all such kinds of false egos completely. Should there be any false ego, *karma* will predominate, not *bhakti*. If we do anything by means of our false ego, vanity, we will get only temporary, mundane benefits. We will become attached to this world. This world is made of matter. Consequently, our minds will become inert like matter. Our minds will have no connection with the spiritual realm. After performing such activities, we will find ourselves in the same position as we were when we first started. We cannot deliver ourselves from the contact of the material things of this world. We cannot get *bhakti* only by moving from place to place and going through the motions. This is not *bhakti*. This is *karma*.

You have to give up every kind of false ego of this world. You must believe, "I am not of this world. This world is unholy." Even the realm of Brahman is unholy. If you think, "I am of the realm of Brahman," then you will become unholy. Thinking in this way, you cannot perform *bhakti*, what to speak of thinking oneself to be a part of this world. I am not of this world, I am not of my family, I am not of London, I am not of Birmingham, I am not of Delhi, I am not of Punjab. These are all unholy. Everything is unholy. If you become unholy, whatever you do will be undone. There should not even be one cent of false ego. How can you do this? It is very difficult.

"*Hari oṁ tat sat*." If I think, "I am of Kṛṣṇa," then I shall become holy, sacred. Then, whatever I do will be for the satisfaction of Śrī Kṛṣṇa. This is properly called *bhakti*. There are sense organs and objects of the sense organs. Without them, we cannot move. But, simply engaging the sense organs and the objects of the sense organs is not *bhakti* if the ego is not correct. Should there be material ego, then the benefit will also be material. By performing devotional practices while deluded by egoistic misconceptions, we will achieve only material benefit. But if we desire eternal, spiritual benefit, we should think, "I am of Kṛṣṇa! I am of the Vaiṣṇavas! I am of the Guru!" Then, we will become holy. If we think like this while engaging the sense organs and the objects of the sense organs, we will actually be practicing the devotional forms.

I shall provide an example. In our social system in Bengal, and here in Vṛndāvana also, the bridegroom and his party would go to the house of the bride for the marriage ceremony. There is so much rainfall in Bengal. So, to go from one place to another, people would take the help of a rowboat, navigating through the rivers. Once, a particular bridegroom and his party boarded a rowboat, along with a helmsman to steer the boat.

The bridegroom said to the pilot, "I need to go to such-and-such place in the dead of night, as the wedding is set for a fixed time tomorrow. We must reach that village no later than 2 AM."

"Oh, that is not far!" the pilot said. "We can reach it by 10 PM. It will not be difficult."

They started on their journey. It was the dark fortnight. The helmsman sat at the front of the boat, rowing with oars. The boat started to move, or at least they thought the boat was moving. A cold breeze was blowing. Everyone became hungry. The bridegroom's party had brought many good dishes for the journey and everyone was fed sumptuously. After eating, they felt drowsy and wanted to go to sleep. The bridegroom reminded the pilot, "Remember that we must be there before 2 AM." The pilot said, "Yes, it is alright," and the party fell asleep.

Everyone slept. When they awoke, it was morning. "Hey! What is this?" the bridegroom cried. He was enraged. "You have spoiled everything! You have not navigated the boat! You have sat idle all night!" A big argument broke out.

"No, no, no!" the pilot protested. "I have been rowing throughout the night. I am perspiring from the effort!"

The party looked about and was shocked to see that no one had lifted the anchor when they had started their journey.

"Oh!" the groom exclaimed. "We are in the same place. We have not moved an inch all night!"

If we think, "I am of this world, I am of this family, I am of London, I am of Delhi, I am of such-and-such family," and other such material egos, we will be anchored to this world. We perform *bhajana* in this state of mind. Throughout our life, we are performing *bhajana* and, at the end, we see that we are at the same place. We have not moved an inch. If we go on doing this for hundreds and thousands of births, we will not succeed in our spiritual endeavors. If, however, we wish, "If only I could be associated with Kṛṣṇa, if only I could serve Him," then the eternal nature of the real self could be imparted to that soul and that fortunate soul would become awakened. This we should do. Only when we say, "I am of Kṛṣṇa," then the real ego will come—the spiritual ego. Then, whatever we do will be *bhakti*.

Bhakti is very difficult for those who have no submissive tendency. They cannot perform *bhakti*. It is easiest for those who have the aptitude for taking shelter of the Supreme Lord and His absolute counterpart, the *śuddha bhakta*. The practice of *bhakti* is simultaneously the easiest and the most difficult process. If there should be the presence of material ego, it will render it impossible to perform *bhak-*

ti. People such as Hiraṇyakaśipu and others could perform immense penances, but they could not perform *bhakti*. They did not want to give up their ego, their vanity. We are a part of the potency of the Supreme Lord, but we are not the Supreme Lord. Why is it that we have become *jīvās* and received this conditioned state, encountering all kinds of difficulties as we pass through countless births and deaths? Would God pass through births and deaths? Obviously, we are not God, the Supreme Lord. We are a part of His potency. We have committed an offense and forgotten our real position. For this reason, the illusory energy has enveloped us and we have assumed these false egos. If we wish to perform pure devotion, then we have to give up these false egos.

During the time of our Guru Mahārāja (Śrīla Bhakti Dayita Mādhava Gosvāmī Mahārāja), a Janmāṣṭamī celebration occurred when there was a scarcity of rice. Even householders could not donate rice to the Maṭha. So, we could take rice at only one meal a day. At the other meals we would take wheat and pound it together with mung dal into a mixture to make a *kitri*—a hodgepodge. Ordinarily, *kitri* is made with rice and dal, not wheat. Those were difficult times. But then, every institution declared that they would not be distributing *kitri* during Janmāṣṭamī, as there was no rice. Generally, we would make a large amount of *kitri*—it is very easy to prepare—and distribute it to thousands of people. But at that time, there was no rice. We prayed to Guru Mahārāja, "Please announce at tonight's Janmāṣṭamī celebration that we will not be celebrating the usual festival with distribution of *kitri* to all tomorrow. Instead, every institution will give sweets instead of *kitri*." Guru Mahārāja said, "Alright, alright."

That evening, at the Janmāṣṭamī function, many distinguished Vaiṣṇavas spoke till about 10:30 PM. At around 11 PM, Guru Mahārāja began his discourse on the chapter of the advent of Śrī Kṛṣṇa from *Śrīmad Bhāgavatam*. After he completed his lecture, he announced, "There will now be *abhiṣeka* for Kṛṣṇa's advent time at midnight. After that, there will be *pūjā,* followed by *bhoga-rāga.* Today, we are observing a fast and may only take some fruits. Tomorrow, Nanda Mahārāja will come to know that he has a Son! So, he will be very glad, and will distribute *prasādam.* So, I invite all of you to come again tomorrow and we shall feed you."

The devotees were astounded. "How can this be? We have no rice!" They knew very well that, in Bengal, if one person were invited, he would bring ten others. So, one thousand invitees instantly become ten thousand. They were perturbed.

Guru Mahārāja went to his room and many of us followed. We asked him, "How can we feed all these people tomorrow? We have no rice."

Then Guru Mahārāja declared, "It is true there is a scarcity of rice. But, nonetheless, we see that everybody is still carrying on celebrating their own marriage ceremonies, birthday ceremonies and the like. Supreme Lord Śrī Kṛṣṇa is the only Master and Enjoyer of these infinite *brahmāṇḍas.* There will be no festival to celebrate His advent? There must be a feast tomorrow!"

I do not know who sent rice, but the next day there was a huge function and all were fed with *kitri.* From where had it come? Who had sent it? We do not have this sort of faith.

There was once a *brahmacārī* from Assam who came to visit our temple in Madhuvana. He lived alone in a very nice, secluded place performing *bhajana.* He used to come to Vṛndāvana to see us whenever Guru Mahārāja was there. He was very simple-hearted and we would always have fun when speaking with him. Once, when he came, we teased him saying, "By remaining alone, you cannot be rescued! You have to serve the Vaiṣṇavas!"

"What am I to do?" he asked.

"We shall all come to stay with you!" There were ten of us saying this to him. "We ten Vaiṣṇavas shall go to your house and remain there for ten days. We Bengalis find it very difficult to digest the kind of bread you eat here, so you will have to get rice, curries, etc., for us."

The *brahmacārī* was in the habit of obtaining his meals by begging alms from the *Vrajavāsis*. They gave him only *roṭi* (bread) and some *gaur* (molasses-like sugar). Only occasionally did he receive some small preparations. "Where shall I get such things?" he protested. But, being very witty, he said, "No, no, no! I shall serve you always! I shall take photographs of all ten Vaiṣṇavas and put them in my temple. Every day I shall make an offering to Giridhāri, then to Gurudeva and then to you, always. But if all of you, in your living forms, come to my house and take so many things, I will not be able to supply it all. It is not possible! I do not want living Vaiṣṇavas, I want to serve 'Photo-Vaiṣṇavas'!"

Photo-Vaiṣṇavas are very easy. Every day, you can serve them. We do not want to be guided or restrained or regulated by Vaiṣṇavas. We are thinking, "If I remain in a secluded place, I can do whatever I desire. I can serve myself and perform *bhajana*." Our Paramgurudeva (Śrīla Bhaktisiddhānta Sarasvatī Prabhupāda) said that this sort of *bhajana* is hypocrisy. It is not befitting behavior for Vaiṣṇavas.

The great Vaiṣṇava saint, Vaṁsī dāsa Bābājī Mahārāja, was no ordinary *sādhu*. Outwardly, he had his advent in what is now known as Bangladesh, in Majidpur Village, Maimansingh district, near Jamālpur. But later, he came to Navadvīpa-dhāma, accepted the *bābājī* order and performed his *bhajana* under a tree. The order of *sannyāsa* is given for preaching, but a *bābājī* will perform *bhajana* in a holy, secluded place. A *bābājī* will not go outside for *pracāra* (preaching). Many people would come to Bābājī Mahārāja and offer to build him a cottage, but he chose to remain always beneath a banyan tree. He would not move from there. He was surcharged with *kṛṣṇa-prema*. He was a very tall figure. He never shaved, but remained like a madman. Many people would offer him various things, but he would pay them no attention. Whatever he might receive, he would distribute to others. He was an anchorite. Nobody could understand his behavior. He had only two big cloth bags—he had no temple. In one cloth bag was Gaura-Nitāi, and in the other, Rādhā-Kṛṣṇa. Sometimes, he would take the Deities out and perform *pūjā*. So, is his *bhakti* less because he had just small Deities, and ours greater because we have a big temple? Gaura-Nityānanda were most satisfied by his service. Our Param Pūjyapāda Bhaktisiddhānta Sarasvatī Ṭhākura used to bow down to him from a distance. He prohibited his disciples from visiting Bābājī Mahārāja. His disciples asked, "Shall we not have *darśana* of the *sādhus*?" But Śrīla Bhaktisiddhānta Sarasvatī Ṭhākura replied, "You will not be able to understand his behavior and you will commit offenses. He is not within this world, but is moving in the transcendental realm. If I commit an offense, it will be anti-devotional. For this reason, I am bowing down to him from a distance. Only a *śuddha bhakta* can understand his wonderful behavior. An ordinary novice of *bhajana* will be unable to understand, so he should not go there. Bābājī Mahārāja is always surcharged with *kṛṣṇa-prema*!"

There was a person from Navadvīpa-dhāma who used to come to Bābājī Mahārāja. One day, he thought, "I have the desire to obtain the Supreme Lord. How can I get Bhagavān?" He was only murmuring, speaking to himself, but Bābājī Mahārāja did not reply. This person came back repeatedly to see Bābājī Mahārāja. Finally, one day, he approached Mahārāja.

"What do you want?" Bābājī Mahārāja asked him.

"I want to see Bhagavān," the man said.

Bābājī Mahārāja replied with only one word: "Weep!"

We might supply so much scriptural evidence to try to explain it in so many ways, but what did Vaṁsī dāsa Bābājī Mahārāja say? "Weep for Him!" If you can weep for Him, then you can get Him. If there is want for Him, then He will come. We are uttering His Names, but we do not want Him. So, we are uttering the Names of Kṛṣṇa—"*hare kṛṣṇa, hare kṛṣṇa, kṛṣṇa kṛṣṇa, hare hare, kṛṣṇa rāma, hare rāma, rāma rāma, hare hare*"—and Kṛṣṇa appears before us. He says to us, "Come along!"

We say to Him, "No, I cannot go now. Right now I require a million dollars to save my business. I have my children. I have just bought a building. I cannot go now."

"So, why have you called Me?" Kṛṣṇa asks.

"I have called you to give me a million dollars," we reply. "Remove my difficulties. I do not have time to go now."

From where are we uttering the Name? Not from the heart! We chant, "*hare kṛṣṇa*," but if Kṛṣṇa comes, we will be unable to go.

A certain Svāmījī gave an illustration. It is an illustration involving the ordinary day-to-day life of a householder but, nonetheless, there is something very impressive about this illustration. In a town in Bengal, there was a man who worked in an office. He lived with his wife and two children. One child was only three or four months old and the other was seven years old. One day, the man told his wife, "You will have to prepare breakfast early today because I have to go into the office early. After I eat, I shall leave right away." When the wife went to cook, she first put the baby on the bed and then went into the kitchen. But whenever she would enter the kitchen, the child would cry. She thought, "With the child in my lap, how will I be able to cook? It is very difficult." She was thinking what she should do. Then she thought of a way she could manage. She called the seven-year-old child.

"Darling, come here!" she called. "Do you know that red toy in the shop?"

"Yes, I know it," the child answered.

"Go and buy that toy, but be sure that it makes a nice jingling sound."

The child took some money and went off to buy the toy. He brought it home and gave it to the mother. The mother laid the baby down on the bed and hung the red-colored toy with the jingling sound above him, at the end of a rope. The baby saw the toy and immediately started to play with it, hitting it from side to side. The child was most delighted as he continued to slap the toy and hear the jingling sound. For one hour he played like that, and the mother went to do her cooking. After that, the child started to feel hungry. For the entire time that the child was playing, he did not remember his mother. But now that he felt hungry, he thought, "Oh, where is my mother?" But his mother did not come. Then, he started crying, signifying, "I am hungry! Come!" He could not speak, so he beckoned his mother by crying. "Come to me and suckle me! I am hungry!"

His mother, however, was busy cooking. "No," she thought, "Let the child cry."

After some time, the child stopped crying and went back to playing with the toy—jingle, jingle, jingle. After playing like that for a while, the pangs of hunger returned. His hunger increased and increased and he became more and more unhappy. He began to cry for his mother even more loudly than before.

His mother heard the crying of the baby, but thought that she should first finish her cooking.

Finally, the hunger became unbearable for the child. The child thought, "I don't want toys!" All he could think about was his mother. His crying became louder and louder until he was screaming. He started to throw his arms about and kick his legs, in a tantrum.

Then the mother thought, "Oh, I cannot stay away any longer!" The mother ran toward the child, embraced him and suckled him.

Like this, the Supreme Lord has given us toys—the toy of a wife or husband, toys of children, toys of buildings, toys of radios, toys of videos, toys of computers. Seeing this, Kṛṣṇa thinks, "They are absorbed in their toys! I have no worries. I am engaged in My pastimes in the transcendental realm. They do not want this. They want those things instead. Here, take this computer! Take that video! Take this! Take that!"

Upon the awakening of his real self (*ātmā*), a man feels the want of the sweetest affection of the Supreme Lord. He cries, "Oh Supreme Lord! In this world, nothing gives me happiness. Everything is temporary. Everyone is selfish. You are my Most Beloved! Where are You? I have forgotten You! Come! Come! I am in a furnace! Come! Come!" Weeping, he calls, but Kṛṣṇa does not come. "I am engaged in My pastimes," Kṛṣṇa says. For some time, the man then becomes absorbed in the affairs of his family and relatives, and forgets Kṛṣṇa. Time passes and he cries again, "Where is My Beloved Supreme Lord? Where is He?" Crying, crying. But, the Supreme Lord still does not come. Ultimately, he shouts, "I do not want a house! I do not want anything! Nobody is mine—You are mine! Oh Beloved Supreme Lord! Come! Come! Come!" He cries and weeps, tossing his arms and legs about. Then Kṛṣṇa cries, "Oh!" and comes to him. This sort of perturbation of the heart, extreme eagerness for getting Bhagavān, must be there.

Vaṁsī dāsa Bābājī Mahārāja said only one word: "Weep!" But, that single word has great significance. When we associate with the *śuddha bhakta* who is crying for Kṛṣṇa, then the eternal nature of *ātmā* will be awakened. You have love for God. Love is there in your soul. It exists, but it is presently enveloped by the external potency of the Supreme Lord and you have become averse to Śrī Kṛṣṇa. Passing through different species, our minds have become enveloped by so many evil desires.

There was once an exhibition at our Calcutta Maṭha. A part of the exhibition was a tightly sealed glass bottle full of honey, covered with bees. The bees were trying to taste the honey through the glass. The narrator explained the significance of the exhibition. If bees, or even human beings, attempt to taste that honey through the transparent covering, they may think that they are actually tasting the honey. But the honey is covered by transparent glass. In reality, they are tasting only glass. There is only one obstacle between the honey and the tongue, but the glass is so transparent, that they are not even aware of its presence. By tasting the transparent glass, they think, "Oh, honey is not sweet at all. I have tasted it. It is sour. It is pungent. It is nothing." What is the taste of glass? Nothing. They believe this because the tongue has not touched the honey itself. But, should that glass be broken, then—oh!

In a similar way, we utter the Name of Bhagavān. It is Complete, Transcendental Ambrosia. But, we are not able to relish the taste because there are so many evil ideas and motives that create an obstruction. We actually only taste our evil motives. We have no connection with the Name itself. So, how can we utter the Holy Name?

Initially, Ajāmila was a staunch *brāhmaṇa*. He was a very good child who had love for his parents and respect for saintly persons. He had all twelve brahminical qualities. So, all his father's money was entrusted to him. But one day, his father ordered him to bring some articles to him in order to perform oblations. He went to the forest to collect the articles, such as *kuśa* grass and sacred wood. On his way back, he saw something obscene: a harlot and a man engaged in illicit sexual activity. Upon seeing this, his mind became perturbed. This obscene event disturbed his mind greatly and, consequently, he felt the urge to associate with the harlot. We should therefore avoid obscene sights. They are a very bad influence for us. After all, why do so many young boys and girls lose their character? By seeing such obscene things. Ajāmila is a good example of this. He tried to control himself, thinking, "I am a *brāhmaṇa*. I should not associate with a prostitute. I am married and have my own wife. My parents are also to be considered." When you try to withdraw the mind from worldly things, those worldly things will come. You may try to think, "I will not think about my wife. I will not think about my children. I will not think about my house." But if you think about Kṛṣṇa, then you engage all your senses in the service of Kṛṣṇa, your mind is for Kṛṣṇa and all the objects of your attachment are given for the service of Kṛṣṇa. Automatically, your attachment to worldly objects goes to the positive side. But if you try to negate things, saying, "I shall not think this, I shall not think that," those things will come. This is not a good procedure.

Ajāmila would secretly go to visit that harlot. He would give her money and enjoy her company. In fact, he spent all his money on her. The prostitute always wanted something or other. "Give me money! Give me ornaments!" she would demand. Eventually, all his money, meant for maintaining his unsuspecting wife and elderly parents, was gone. He left his home and went to live with the prostitute and, for her satisfaction, performed all kinds of sinful activities and crimes, such as theft and robbery.

Ajāmila fathered ten sons in the womb of the harlot. By dint of his previous good status, he named the youngest son Nārāyaṇa, who was born when Ajāmila was eighty-eight years old. Ajāmila had great affection for this youngest son. He always had firm attachment to that beautiful, small boy. He was attracted to his every move and word. He would call to the boy, "Oh darling, come here. You should not go there or you will fall down." He walked with him, slept with him and ate with him. It was always, "Nārāyaṇa! Nārāyaṇa! Nārāyaṇa! Nārāyaṇa!"

But soon, the time for Ajāmila's death arrived. Up until that point, he had been completely absorbed and engrossed in worldly matters. He did not even realize that his ultimate end had come. He saw three messengers of the god of death (Yāmarāja) approaching. They were horrible figures, with fiery eyes and brown hairs that stood straight up on their heads. Significantly, there were three messengers because every person of this world commits sin in three ways: by words, body and mind (thoughts, words and deeds). So, at the time of death, three messengers will appear.

There is still one person living in Navadvīpa-dhāma today who saw Yāma-purī—the realm of the god of death. He was taken there by mistake. After seeing that he had died, his family took him to the cremation ground for burning. But, when they arrived there, people noticed some movement in his body. Suddenly he sat up.

The people asked, "Are you a ghost?"

"No, I am not a ghost!" he said.

"What happened?" they asked.

"I was taken to the realm of Yāmarāja by the messengers of death. They were judging me, stabbing me with pointed spears, injuring me, giving me pain. When it was my time to be judged, they put me before Yāmarāja in his court. When he saw me, he said, 'No, no, no. This man will live to be seventy-eight. You have made a mistake.' The messengers left me and so I have come back here. What I have seen is horrible—I will not remain in my house."

After this experience, he left and searched, wondering, "Where to go? Where to go?" Eventually, he went to Navadvīpa where our Paramgurudeva was staying at the time.

"What have I seen?" the man asked Paramgurudeva.

"You have seen the realm of the god of death. After death, you will be taken there for punishment."

"No! I shall not return there! How can I get help for this?"

"You should perform *harināma*!"

He still lives in Navadvīpa today.

This is not mythology. The government of the Supreme Lord is a reality. The three messengers of the god of death take souls by thrusting them into another subtle covering, a painful covering. That subtle covering is then taken to the realm of Yāmarāja. At that critical moment, Ajāmila could only think of his son, Nārāyaṇa. Ajāmila saw the Yāmadūtas (the messengers of Yāmarāja) and, out of intense fear, shouted, "Nārāyaṇa! Nārāyaṇa!" Then, as he uttered the four syllables of the Name "Nā-rā-ya-ṇa", four associates of Nārāyaṇa, all resembling Nārāyaṇa, each possessing four arms, holding a conch shell, disc, club and lotus flower, appeared before him. They were very beautiful. They stopped the messengers of Yāmarāja, shouting,

"Stop! Why are you taking this man?"

Then the messengers of the god of death said, "Your appearance is very beautiful. Perhaps you are demigods. Perhaps you are *ṛṣis* or *munis*. But you are not doing any good by interfering. We are the servants of the god of death and we have come here upon his order. You do not know that this man was originally a good *brāhmaṇa*. He used to serve his parents and he had devotion to his Gurudeva. He was always very well behaved and full of good qualities. But once, when his father sent him to get some articles for sacrifice, he witnessed an obscene sight to which he became attracted. He then spent all his father's money in the association of a harlot. He left his parents destitute. How will they manage in their old age? He did not even think about this. He also left his duly married wife. He committed many crimes, such as theft and robbery and he has not done anything for atonement of these sins. So, we are taking him for retribution. Why are you objecting?"

Then, the very beautiful personal associates of Nārāyaṇa replied, "He has uttered the Name of Nārāyaṇa! He has made expiation not merely for one birth, but for crores (tens of millions) of births! All his sins have been destroyed. This is only *nāma-abhāsa*—a glimpse of the Name. The rays of the sun, coming directly from the sun, reflect in a tank of water. When that reflection shines on you, it is called *abhāsa*. When this man, Ajāmila, called to his son, Nārāyaṇa, the utterance went directly to Nārāyaṇa Himself—*nāma-abhāsa*. He uttered the Name 'Nārāyaṇa.' Even if a person, being unable to utter the whole Name, utters only 'Nā'—any part of Infinity—he will gain benefit. This man uttered 'Nārāyaṇa!' All his sins from crores and crores of births and deaths have been destroyed. He has been rescued and has attained salvation. So, why are you taking a pure heart to punish? Where will people go to take shelter if Dharmarāja (Yām arāja) is doing such things? He is punishing someone who is pure and completely divested of all sins. What type of crimes has he committed?

stenaḥ surā-po mitra-dhrug
brahma-hā guru-talpa-gaḥ
strī-rāja-pitṛ-go-hantā
ye ca pātakino 'pare

sarveṣām apy aghavatām
idam eva suniṣkṛtam
nāma-vyāharaṇaṁ viṣṇor
yatas tad-viṣayā matiḥ
(Śrīmad Bhāgavatam, 6.2.9-10)

Committing theft is a sin. If one steals valuables, gold, etc., it is a great sin. If one takes drugs or intoxicants, that is also sinful. If one kills a human being, that is certainly a great sin, but if I kill a man who has placed his trust in me, that is an even greater sin. Killing a *brāhmaṇa* or having an illicit connection with a woman are also sinful deeds. But, having an illicit connection with the wife of one's superiors, such as an elder brother, is an even more serious crime. The killing of one's wife or parents, the killing of the king, who is protecting us—all these heinous crimes, one may have performed. One may have committed any of these sinful acts, but by uttering His Name, God responds. 'Who is calling My Name? I will come to that person!' When He comes to that person, all sins are destroyed. There are no sins in this man. You should not take him."

It is said at the conclusion of the story of Ajāmila in *Śrīmad Bhāgavatam*:

mriyamāṇo harer nāma
gṛṇan putropacāritam
ajāmilo 'py agād dhāma
kim uta śraddhayā gṛṇan
(Śrīmad Bhāgavatam, 6.2.49)

At the time of death, at the age of eighty-eight years, Ajāmila, due to his fear at seeing the horrible figures of the messengers of the god of death, thinking about his son, uttered the Name: "Nārāyaṇa!" He was rescued. So, those who utter the Name with great faith, with firm faith—how can we estimate the extent of their benefit? Nobody can. Ajāmila was certainly a great sinner, but he had become pure. He had been divested of all the contamination of sin. If such a great sinner became sanctified, how can we possibly chant the glories of those who perform *harināma* with great faith?

Actually, our position is even worse than that of Ajāmila's. The western devotees have changed their custom and now give their sons the names of Bhagavān, such as "Kṛṣṇa and "Rāma"." They now give their daughters the names of the internal potency of the Supreme Lord, such as "Rādhā." But, nowadays in India, in many places, you will find that parents are now giving their sons and daughters worldly names. We ask them, "You have given up the heritage of your forefathers, who gave their sons and daughters the names of Bhagavān, the Supreme Lord. Why are you doing this? What have you called your son?"

"Pinky!" one person replied.

So, that child has the name "Pinky." His parents love him very much. They are always thinking, "Pinky, come here. Pinky, come here." They move with Pinky; they eat with Pinky; they sleep with Pinky—Pinky, Pinky, Pinky. Then, when the messengers of the god of death come, out of fear they will cry, "Pinky!" and the messengers will take them. If they were to call out "Govinda," "Nārāyaṇa," "Rāmacandra," "Rādhā-Ramaṇa," etc., they could be saved.

Keep the Name. Then, at the time of death, if you utter the Name of the Supreme Lord, you will go to Vaikuṇṭha.

Kṛṣṇa, The Greatest Magician

Today we are present at the "Mountain Temple Center" in Phoenix. I have heard from the devotees that someone here is a magician. Is there a magician here? (*The owner of the center acknowledges that he is a magician*). You are the magician? Oh! You see, everything is done by the will of the Supreme Lord. Without His will, nothing can be done. If anybody says, "Yes, I can do something against the will of the Supreme Lord, then the Supreme Lord will lose His absolute position. Even a leaf cannot move without His approval. So, why have I been brought here to this Mountain Temple Center, where the owner is a magician? For what reason has God sent us here? There is some purpose to it. By this, the Supreme Lord is teaching us that wherever we are staying in this world is the result of the magic of the Supreme Lord. We are already seeing magic. Whatever we are seeing around us is jugglery. Is it not true? And within this world, a tiny godlike being is also displaying magic. Is that not also true? Who, however, is the Greatest Magician? The Supreme Lord, Śrī Kṛṣṇa. Everything we are seeing here is His magic. When you see magic, you take it to be real. But, actually, it is illusion—false.

Many years ago, when I first came to Śrī Caitanya Maṭha in Śrī Māyāpura, Navadvīpa-dhāma, India, I heard a story about a famous magician who had come to Māyāpura to perform his magic. The Maṭha was packed with visitors, not only from Śrī Māyāpura, but from other places as well. Arrangements were made for the seating of all the visitors. The magician arrived at the full house, accompanied by two or three assistants. Before he began his first feat of magic, he told the audience, "You should not be frightened by what you are about to witness. I am going to take this saw and cut someone from the audience in half. By the grace of the Lord, no mishap will come to him. He will be fine." He brought out a box and a volunteer from the audience came up to lie down inside it. "Don't be frightened," he repeated, "everything will be okay." Then, two of the assistants picked up a huge saw, placed it over the middle of the box and began to saw through it. After some time, they had sawn through the box. The box was in two halves. There was blood spilling onto the floor and the audience became alarmed. It appeared that the person inside the box had been killed. Many expressed fear that the police would come and arrest them. Many people began to flee.

"Don't go! Don't be afraid!" the magician cried to them. "Why are you afraid? You are *sādhus*. By your grace, this man will be all right. Have no fear."

But many of the audience still thought, "This man has been killed—we should not remain here. How can we remain here when the man's blood is pouring out?"

Ultimately, the magician exclaimed, "Come!" He uttered some incantation and then, shouting, commanded the dead man, "Rise up!" The crowd was astounded to see the man rise up, completely well.

Of course, it was all an illusion. The magician appeared to be sawing the person in half, but there was some sort of trick going on. In actuality, he did not even touch the man. Outside persons could not see the trick. Even the *sādhus* had become frightened upon seeing this illusion of the magician. What to speak of this magician and his audience, Supreme Lord Śrī Kṛṣṇa performs His own great magical display of infinite planets, and all are enchanted by His magic.

Recently, when we were in Singapore, the person hosting our trip wanted to show us the island of Sentosa. We were to cross the ocean by boat to the island and then return later that day in order to go to a program somewhere else that evening. He told us that there were various things to be seen there. Visitors from all over the world come to visit that island. I agreed to go on the condition that we should return well before that evening's function. "If we travel very far," I said, "we will be too tired when we return, having had no time to take rest." Our friend assured us not to worry and that there would be plenty of time. So, we left for Sentosa. We were brought to various places and saw many sights. Ultimately, we were taken to a cinema. When I was a young person living at my parents' house, on principle, I would never go to any cinema. In all my years in Calcutta, even when I was young at University, I had never once entered a cinema, on principle. In Calcutta, there are the very famous Zoological Gardens, and many people said I should go there. "Oh, the whole world goes to see these gardens," people would tell me. "For what reason should I go?" I thought. Nowadays, people come to our Maṭha, and the first thing they go to see is the Zoological Gardens, but I have never seen them. I have always been this type of person. But now our host had brought us to this cinema house.

(The wind gets very strong at this point and starts to blow over the candles and pictures. Mahārāja says, "This is one kind of magic.")

This cinema house was like a stadium. We sat there and someone came and fastened a seatbelt around my waist. This was strange. I asked, "You are showing a film. Why are you fastening a seatbelt around my waist?" "You might fall down," I was told. "Why?" I asked. Then they switched off the lights to that grand stadium. Everything became dark and the film began.

I thought to myself, "What am I doing here? I have renounced household life to worship the Supreme Lord. Is this some form of worship?"

As I sat, they were showing the film. There were trucks running very fast along the road. In front of them, there was a motorcycle speeding along in such a way that there could have been an accident at any moment. "Why are they showing this?" I wondered. After some time, the motorcycle and one of the trucks moved in such a way that it seemed as if there would surely be a collision. At this point, as we were sitting there, the whole stadium started to rumble. We looked at each other. "Are we moving?" we wondered. We thought, "We are moving so fast along the roads and through the countryside! There will definitely be an accident. This is why they fastened our waists! We are moving so fast, but where are we going?"

Eventually, in front of us, we saw some gasoline tanks. "Oh," we thought, "this time we will surely crash!"

But the stadium continued to move at high speed. Running at this rate, it felt to us that perhaps, by now, we had left Singapore for some distant destination. If this were so, then it would not be possible for us to attend the evening program.

Ultimately, we were brought to the seashore. I thought, "Definitely we will be unable to attend the program tonight!"

Then, the lights to the stadium were switched on and we could see that we were in the stadium. What had we seen? This was the magic of human beings. Actually, we had not been moving at all, but they had made it appear so. At the time it was going on, we could not understand this. Then the manager of the theatre announced that they would be starting another show wherein a person would be lifted up and then he would fall down from a great height. Everyone cried, "No! We don't want to see this lest we be killed by having a heart attack!"

Ha! The human being's jugglery! Magic! We are infatuated upon seeing this. But Supreme Lord Śrī Kṛṣṇa is performing His great magic of the creation of infinite planets and all are enchanted by His magic. Even in our scriptures you will find evidence of this. Mārkeṇḍeya Ṛṣi performed immense penance and received boons from Mahādeva (Śiva) and from Badarinārāyaṇa Viṣṇu. The demigods along with their king, Indra, tried to break Mārkeṇḍeya's penance by alluring him with various temptations. But Mārkeṇḍeya Ṛṣi always remained very calm and serene. They had never seen such a person before. They were unable to create any restlessness of mind in him. All the demigods, including Mahādeva, were astounded. Mahādeva, along with Nārāyaṇa, appeared before him. Badarinārāyaṇa said to him, "I am satisfied by your austerities. Tell me what it is you wish."

"I want to see Your *māyā*!" Mārkeṇḍeya Ṛṣi said.

"All right, then, you shall see it!" said Nārāyaṇa affirmatively.

That *muni* had been performing meditation in front of his cottage. All of a sudden, he saw a storm. The air started to blow, increasing and increasing. The whole sky became consumed with clouds. Soon, the rains began. The land became completely inundated with water. Continuously there was rain, rain, rain and his cottage was also soon covered with water. He watched as he saw everything of this world become immersed in a vast sea. He might have drowned in this sea, but he had previously received a boon from Brahmā that he would survive for seven *kalpas*. One *kalpa* is one day of Brahmā. So, his boon was to live for seven days of Brahmā, not seven earth days as we know them today. You cannot mentally fathom the mathematical calculation of such a high figure.

Presently, we are in this black age of Kali-yuga. The span of time for this Kali-yuga is 432,000 years. Double of this (864,000 years) is the duration of the Dvāpara-yuga. Triple of the Kali-yuga (1,296,000 years) is the duration of the Tretā-yuga and quadruple it (1,728,000 years) is the length of the Satya-yuga, the "Golden Age." If you add the total time of these four *yugas* together, the sum is 4,320,000 years. If the span of time covered by these four ages is multiplied by seventy-one (306,720,000), then that is the span of life of one Manu. The fourteen Manus are sons of Brahmā, and are called "Manu" because they were created by the mind of Brahmā. The total number of years in which the lives of fourteen Manus have passed, (14 X 306,720,000 = 4,294,080,000 years) equals one day of Brahmā. Such seven days (30,058,560,000 years) would be the lifespan of Mārkeṇḍeya Ṛṣi. How did he get such a boon?

Mṛkaṇḍa had learned from an astrologer that his son, Mārkeṇḍeya, would die at the age of ten. So, he was in a very melancholy state. He could find no peace of mind. "Here is my only son," he thought, "and that son will die at the age of ten?" He went to his son and instructed him, "Whenever any elder person comes to see you, you should bow down to him. You should make prostrated obeisances to him." As per the instruction of his father, whenever an elder person of respectable stature came to their house, Mārkeṇḍeya made prostrated obeisances to him.

By chance, the Saptārṣis (the seven *ṛṣis*), also the sons of Brahmā, set their holy footprints in the house of the descendents of Bhṛgu, and the boy, Mārkeṇḍeya, fell flat at their feet.

The *ṛṣis* blessed him. "May he live eternally!" they exclaimed.

The boy's father was astonished. He approached the *ṛṣis* and said, "But my son is destined to die at the age of ten. Now you have given him a boon, but will this boon be effective?"

"Oh, is that true?" the *ṛṣis* asked. They were perturbed because they wanted to award the child some sort of boon. They took the boy to Satya-loka, the planet of Brahmā. They told their father, "We went to this boy's house only to set our holy footprints there and this boy, out of affection, fell flat at our feet. He is unfortunately destined to live ten years only."

"No!" cried Brahmā. "His span of life is seven days—of mine!" Thus, Brahmā gave him this boon.

We should never ignore our superiors. We are learning this lesson from the son of Mṛkaṇḍa, Mārkeṇḍeya Ṛṣi. If we bow down to parents, elders, Vaiṣṇavas and *sādhus*, then by their grace, we shall be able to get things we cannot imagine. Mārkeṇḍeya is one such example.

So, when Mārkeṇḍeya requested to see *māyā*, the illusion of the Supreme Lord, clouds, followed by heavy rainfall, suddenly surrounded his cottage. The whole area had become inundated and had become a sea, an ocean. But, due to his boon, he did not die. There were whales, sharks and other creatures swimming in the water, attacking and wounding him, but he did not die. At that time, he thought, "Why have I obtained this span of life? It would be better if I were to die!"

He drifted in this way through this vast ocean for one thousand years. After that, he drifted to Puruṣottama-dhāma (Purī, Orissa). There, he saw a banyan tree. A leaf of the banyan tree was floating on the waters of the great sea. A small boy—very attractive—was seated on that leaf. He thought, "Where has this boy come from? He is so attractive!" He came closer. Mārkeṇḍeya, seeking shelter from the aquatic animals that were attacking him, approached the beautiful boy.

This very wonderful boy was inhaling and exhaling. When Mārkeṇḍeya came close to the nostrils of the boy, he entered into one of the nostrils as the boy inhaled, thereby entering into the body of the boy. Within the body of the boy, he saw mountains, hills, birds and all created beings. He saw houses and human beings. For one thousand years, he passed the time in this fashion. The boy then exhaled. Mārkeṇḍeya was expelled from the nostril and he again felt as though he were drowning in the devastating ocean. Again, for many years, he underwent great suffering. Again, he thought, "Oh! Why have I obtained this span of life? It would be better if I were to die!"

Again, he saw the beautiful boy and felt attracted to him. Mārkeṇḍeya swam near him, intending to embrace the boy. But the moment he went to embrace the boy, the boy disappeared and Mārkeṇḍeya found himself sitting in front of his cottage, meditating, just as he had been before.

This is magic—the magic of the Supreme Lord. We are also seeing this magic. Presently, we see all the created beings. During the day of Brahmā, everything is created. During the night of Brahmā, everything dissolves. Actually, our real self does not die. It always remains. But we are seeing this creation and destruction—this is the illusion of the Supreme Lord.

Whenever we forget the Supreme Lord, this illusion will envelop us. Even Nārada Gosvāmī was enchanted and infatuated by seeing Kṛṣṇa's *māyā*. We revere Nārada as an *ācārya* in our preceptorial channel. By his grace, we can cross over this ocean of births and deaths. But once, Śrī Nārada himself requested Kṛṣṇa to show him His *māyā*.

Nārada said, "I have heard that all the living beings of this world are experiencing immense miseries due to Your *māyā*—Your illusion—the external potency. I want to see that illusion and know what kind of afflictions they are undergoing."

"You do not want this," Kṛṣṇa told him. "You will become charmed, enchanted. Why do you want to see this illusion? You are singing My glories. You are chanting My Holy Name. You are rescuing all the fallen souls. What benefit will you get by seeing My illusion? You will become infatuated!"

Nārada implored Kṛṣṇa, "If You think that I have the slightest drop of devotion for You, please show me Your *māyā*." Nārada was very obstinate and stubborn about it. You will find this story in Brahma-Vaivarta Purāṇa.

Immediately, Kṛṣṇa turned Himself into a *brāhmaṇa*. Nārada also became a *brāhmaṇa* and his vina, which he always carried, disappeared. No one was able to recognize that this *brāhmaṇa* was Nārada and that the other was Kṛṣṇa.

In Śvetadvīpa, there are many planets. Kṛṣṇa and Nārada were traveling throughout these planets. After many travels, they came to the house of a *vaiśya*. In order that they may obtain devotion, this mercantile class of people serves the *brāhmaṇas*. They utilize their money and other assets to serve the *brāhmaṇas* and the demigods. When Śrī Kṛṣṇa and Nārada Gosvāmī set Their holy footprints in his house, the businessman paid respect to Them. He bowed down and worshipped Them, serving Them very nicely. Kṛṣṇa, in the form of a *brāhmaṇa*, blessed him, saying, "May your wealth increase!" The *vaiśya* was pleased, believing that a *brāhmaṇa* had blessed him. He did not realize that this *brāhmaṇa* was Kṛṣṇa, Himself. Nārada observed Kṛṣṇa's actions with interest.

Kṛṣṇa and Nārada left the house and continued to roam. After many travels, They became the guest of a *brāhmaṇa*. That *brāhmaṇa* also adored Them and served Them nicely. But, at the time of leaving his house, Kṛṣṇa, still in the form of a *brāhmaṇa*, cursed Their host, saying, "May all your wealth be destroyed!" Nārada was perplexed. He wondered, "This man has also served us well. Is Kṛṣṇa showing His magic to me? He has given a boon to the businessman, while He is cursing this *brāhmaṇa*. Why, has He done this, when this *brāhmaṇa* served us so well?"

After they left the house, he complained to Kṛṣṇa. "What are you doing?" he asked. "What is Your reason for this sort of behavior? You should be equal to all! Why have You cursed this man?"

Then Kṛṣṇa replied, "In spite of being a *brāhmaṇa*, this man is engaged in the cultivation of crops—the work of a farmer. He should be engaged in the worship of God only. He should read the Vedas, etc. He should help others to get devotion. He should not have the desire to increase his wealth. If a *brāhmaṇa* ploughs the land for one day, the same degree of sin is incurred as when a fisherman kills fish for an entire year! This *brāhmaṇa* should not be engaged in farming. He should not have this sort of aptitude. I have cursed him for the sake of his eternal welfare."

They traveled onward and Kṛṣṇa thought to Himself, "No matter whether I appear in the form of a *brāhmaṇa*, a *vaiśya* or any other form, Nārada's devotion to Me is always there. If he does not forget Me, how can I show him My magic? In order to accomplish this, he will need to forget Me."

Then, immediately, by His desire, the Supreme Lord, within Whom all the planets are residing, transported Himself and Nārada to this world. No airplane is required. No Sputnik is required. That is magic. When they arrived in this world, They saw a very beautiful lake. The fragrance of lotus flowers was emanating from it. There were numerous varieties of fish swimming in its waters. Birds were flying overhead and swans were swimming about. The water was very clean and clear. Nārada suggested that They perform their ablutions there in the sweet, pure waters of that lake. They had been traveling such a long time and this would refresh them.

Kṛṣṇa told Nārada to go on ahead and take his bath and that He would wait on the shore in the meantime. Nārada entered the water and started to bathe. When he raised his head out of the water, Kṛṣṇa had disappeared. The lake had now become a sea. Nārada's body had transformed into the body of a very beautiful woman. He stayed afloat on the surface by catching hold of a piece of timber. He looked about in all directions. "Oh, everything is water, water!" he lamented. "Who will rescue me? Who will rescue me?" Nārada had forgotten Kṛṣṇa.

Now, the magic of Kṛṣṇa began.

So long as Nārada remembered Kṛṣṇa, there was no magic. But now he was crying, "Who will rescue me? Who will rescue me?" Kṛṣṇa is the only Protector. We should take absolute shelter at the Lotus Feet of Kṛṣṇa. Kṛṣṇa will rescue us. But Nārada had forgotten. So, when we also forget this, then the magic will start! We are presently seeing Kṛṣṇa's magic.

Then, by the desire of Kṛṣṇa, a king named Tāladhvaja appeared. It is said in the scriptures that our birth, death and marriage are all pre-ordained. Everything is done by the will of the Supreme Lord. Therefore, this king had come and Nārada, in the form of a beautiful woman, was beckoning him, signaling him to come and rescue her.

The king thought, "This woman is so beautiful! What has happened to her? Perhaps her boat capsized and all of her traveling companions died." He sent his own boat to her and brought her back to shore.

"Tell me," he asked her, "where do you live? I have never seen such a beautiful woman. Wherever it is that you live, I shall bring you home."

"I do not know where I am from," said Nārada.

"What about your parents?" the king asked.

"I do not know," said Nārada, "please give me shelter."

The king was astounded. He thought, "Perhaps all of her relatives have perished at sea and she is now in a state of shock. Let me take her to my palace."

He brought her to his palace, but she could not regain any memory of her home or family. The king, by watching her beautiful, charming form, eventually desired to marry the woman. Nārada now became queen of a wealthy kingdom. So much land, so many houses, so many elephants, horses, servants, maidservants and ornaments! The queen was always busy serving her husband and became engrossed in all the matters of family life. There were also many temples and many people were engaged in arranging religious events. They would come to the queen and request her to please attend.

"No, I have no time!" she would say. "I am engaged."

In the form of that woman, what was Nārada Muni saying? "I'm engaged. I've got no time to go to the temple of Śrī Kṛṣṇa. You may make my offerings of flowers to the Lotus Feet of the Lord on my behalf."

After ten years, he begat (or, rather, she begat) fifty very beautiful children. At first, she had had love only for her husband, but now the husband and children were sharing her love. When the children reached adulthood, the queen requested that her husband give them some sort of work so that they could increase their wealth.

"My sons?" asked the king, "What will they do? Why do they require money? They will only sit idle. Let them become minor kings instead. I shall divide this property into fifty portions and each son will be a subordinate king."

Originally, all the sons lived with their parents, but now some lived nearby while others lived some distance away. Now, the mother desired that her sons take wives. So, very soon, in a grand way, all fifty sons were married. It was a pompous affair and millions and millions of dollars were spent. Shortly after the wives went to live with their husbands, quarrels between the brothers started to arise. The wives would say to their husbands, "Your elder brother has been given more property than you. Go to your father and ask him to give you more." At first, the sons would say, "Be silent. You should not speak this way. We should be satisfied with whatever our father gives us." But every day, the young wives would continue to press this issue with their husbands. In this way, after some time, the sons began to think, "My wife is actually right." Eventually, one of the brothers went to his father and said, "Why have you given my elder brother more land than I?"

The king implored, "You can see that all that was once mine now belongs to all of you. Why are you quarreling? It is impossible to divide the land of this kingdom into precisely equal portions."

But, in spite of this, the sons went to war among themselves. As a result of their fighting, all fifty sons were killed.

The queen went mad. She had great affection for her children. One after another, she saw her sons die. It was so shocking. The queen, in her grief, now started to blame Kṛṣṇa for this disaster.

"Kṛṣṇa is unkind to the living beings of the world!" she cried. "He is always cruel! He finds His satisfaction in giving afflictions to the living beings! I don't believe Kṛṣṇa is all-good—He is cruel!"

She continued, "He has no knowledge in His brain! We are old men and women, but instead of taking our lives, he is taking the lives of our children! So now, there is no one left to beget children! There will be no children and all creation will be stopped. There is no wisdom in the head of this Creator! He is a dunderhead!"

She wept, due to her separation grief for her sons.

At that time, Kṛṣṇa, in the form of a *brāhmaṇa*, came to her house. "Are you all quite well?" He inquired.

"No!" she wailed. "We have lost all our children! We are in great misery!"

Kṛṣṇa asked her, "Wherefrom have you gotten these children? All living beings are born by the will of the Supreme Lord. They remain here for some time and, when the Supreme Lord desires, He will take them from this world. They do not belong to you. If any of these children had actually belonged to you, then you could have kept that child with you but everything is coming from the Supreme Lord:

jātasya hi dhruvo mṛtyur
dhruvaṁ janma mṛtasya ca
tasmād aparihārye 'rthe
na tvaṁ śocitum arhasi
(Bhagavad-gītā, 2.27)

Why are you mourning? One who has been born will die. It is inevitable. We should not be distressed by this." In this way Kṛṣṇa advised the queen.

Hearing the words of the *brāhmaṇa*, the queen became calmed for a while and stopped weeping. But, after some time, when she would happen to see some garment or other article belonging to one of her sons, she would begin to cry again.

Kṛṣṇa then said to her, "You cannot bring back your children. Please go to the lake and perform ablutions and then come back here to Me. I shall make some arrangements to assure that the departed souls of your sons will find peace."

"I don't want to live in this world!" the queen wailed. "You are a *brāhmaṇa*, so I will abide by your order. But actually, I request that you bless me so that I shall die!"

Nārada, in the form of the queen, followed the instructions of Kṛṣṇa, in the form of a *brāhmaṇa*. He went to the lake to perform ablutions. As he emerged from the water, his eyes fell upon Śrī Kṛṣṇa.

"What are You doing here?" Nārada asked Kṛṣṇa.

"Why don't you tell Me what you have seen?" Kṛṣṇa asked.

"What I have seen," Nārada said, "is very shameful! My body was changed. I became a woman. A king came along and I became his queen. I had a great kingdom with every kind of wealth—servants, elephants, horses, and property. After some time, I had fifty children. I was engrossed in their upbringing. Later, they married. When the wives went to live with them, all the sons began to quarrel among themselves. Then, they fought one another and all the sons were killed. I then rebuked You, saying, "You are cruel! You have no compassion for me! You are a fool! You are stupid! Please, tell me, what is this that I have seen?"

"This is My *māyā*!" Kṛṣṇa replied. "Do you want to see more?"

"No! No!" Nārada cried.

As long as we remember the Supreme Lord and we chant His Name, no *māyā* will come. When we forget Him, then this *māyā* will come. If you see that this person is crying, this person is laughing, this person is doing something else, all these things are illusion. They have no actual existence.

In order to get this knowledge, Kṛṣṇa has brought us to this place—the house of a magician. Can we perform such magic?

So, let us chant the Holy Name—Kṛṣṇa's Name. The Name and the Named are the same. If we chant the Holy Name, the Supreme Lord, Who is All-Existence, All-Knowledge and All-Bliss, will appear and all *māyā* will go. Here, in the company of the *sādhus*, we should remember that whenever we forget Kṛṣṇa, *māyā* will come. So we should take a vow never to forget Him. In this way we will be rescued from *māyā*.

Answers For All Time

We belong to Śrī Caitanya Mahāprabhu's school of thought: pure devotion to Śrī Kṛṣṇa. What are the teachings of Śrī Caitanya Mahāprabhu? One renowned saint, Śrīnātha Cakravartī, has summarized the teachings of Lord Caitanya Mahāprabhu in a nutshell in this verse:

ārādhyo bhagavān vrajeśa-tanayas
tad-dhāma vṛndāvanaṁ
ramyā kācid upāsanā vraja-vadhū-
vargena yā kalpitā
śrimad-bhāgvataṁ pramāṇam amalaṁ
premā pumartho mahān
śrī caitanya-mahāprabhur matam idaṁ
tatrādaro naḥ paraḥ
(from Caitanya-manjusa, a commentary on Śrīmad Bhāgavatam)

"*Ārādhyo bhagavān vrajeśa-tanayas*": Caitanya Mahāprabhu has taught us to worship Kṛṣṇa, the son of Nanda Mahārāja. According to Caitanya Mahāprabhu, Kṛṣṇa, the son of Nanda Mahārāja, is the highest object of worship—the Supreme Lord. "*Tad-dhāma vṛndāvana*": His transcendental, spiritual realm is Vṛndāvana. What form of *bhakti* is foremost there? The *vraja-gopīs*, or milk women of Vraja-maṇḍala, worship Śrī Kṛṣṇa with all their senses and all the objects of their senses. Their worship is unparalleled. No one else can worship in such a manner, as do the *vraja-gopīs*. You will find this evidence in the quintessence of all scriptures, *Śrīmad Bhāgavatam*. What is the ultimate goal of human life? *Kṛṣṇa-prema*. *Dharma*, *artha, kāma* and *mokṣa* are not the ultimate targets for human beings. "*Dharma*" means performing many actions, for our own worldly benefit here and hereafter, as per the instructions of the scriptures. That *dharma* performed with the aim of receiving benefit in this world, in other worlds or after death is not our ultimate goal of life. "*Artha*" means to amass money and "*kāma*" means to fulfill our sensual desires. These are not the ultimate goals of a human being. Even *mukti* (*mokṣa*), deliverance from the cycle of births and deaths, is not our ultimate goal. A prisoner may be released from prison, but after that, what does he get? A prisoner may be granted deliverance or emancipation, but if after that he gets nothing, if he does not become rich, what is his situation? He is free, but what does he have? At first, he was in an undesirable state, in bondage. Now he is released from bondage, but what is he getting after he is released? It is an important point. So, merely getting deliverance from the cycles of *māyā* cannot be the ultimate goal. After that, what shall we get? Love of God—*kṛṣṇa-prema*. That is wealth. If I become released from my debts, that does not mean that I have become rich. I was in debt for the sum of one million dollars and then I paid it back. I can be said to be rich only to the extent of what I may receive after that debt is paid. So, when we get positive things, such as love for Kṛṣṇa, that is called "wealth." That is our requirement: *kṛṣṇa-prema*.

There is a question that is often raised. In several places we have been asked this same question. "Svāmījī Mahārāja, you are saying that *kṛṣṇa-prema* is the ultimate goal of life. But there are many views in this world—many tenets, many "isms", many creeds. Others are also speaking on the evidence of scriptures, but they do not support your view. So we have our doubts. All these teachers are saints and you are also a saint. There are many minds and many views. What shall we do? So many different views of so many sages exist and, for an ordinary person, it is difficult to determine which view we should accept and which view we should disregard."

Human life is very short and people are confused. So, some people ask this question. However, you will find that there is nobody in India, or at least no followers of *sanātana-dharma*, who do not have belief in *Mahābhārata* or *Rāmāyaṇa*. All schools of thought in India have accepted these two literatures and are, therefore, unified in this respect. *Bhagavad-gītā* is, itself, one section of *Mahābhārata*. So, I shall give an item of evidence from *Mahābhārata*. To answer this important question, I am not giving any evidence from *Bhāgavata* (*Śrīmad Bhāgavatam*), as some might object, thinking it to represent a specific viewpoint. If you have any objection that I am giving evidence from *Mahābhārata*, if you do not believe *Mahābhārata*, then you are not a *sanātanī* (a follower of *sanātana-dharma*). If you are not a *sanātanī*, then you do not believe in the *Gītā*, a part of the *Mahābhārata*. It is a big topic, and although it is not possible to narrate it so concisely, I shall try to relate it briefly.

After being defeated in gambling at a game of dice by the Kauravas, the Pāṇḍavas were banished from their kingdom and exiled to the forest for twelve years. After that period, they were to spend one more year incognito, during which time, if anyone recognized them, they would have to spend yet another twelve years in the forest. During the time of their exile in the forest, they first went to Dvaitavana. But when they saw that all the beasts there, especially the deer, were being assassinated, they became very distressed. They left that place and went to Kāmya-vana, within Vraja-maṇḍala. We visit this place when we perform Vraja-maṇḍala *parikrama* (circumambulation). At Kāmya-vana, they experienced another mishap. Jayadhrata, the King of Sindhu, abducted Draupadī. So, there followed a battle between the Pāṇḍavas and Jayadhrata. Through the efforts of Bhīma, Arjuna, etc., the Pāṇḍavas defeated Jayadhrata and rescued Draupadī. At that point, they felt that they should not remain in Kāmya-vana, and henceforth returned to Dvaitavana.

At Dvaitavana, the Pāṇḍavas lived beneath a tree. A *brāhmaṇa* also dwelt in that forest. This *brāhmaṇa* used to perform daily oblations by pouring ghee into a sacred fire, and thusly was referred to as an "*agni-hotri-brāhmaṇa*". At that time, matchsticks were not considered holy for the lighting of these special fires and were, therefore, not used in the performance of *yajñas* (sacrifices). There is a special sacred wood by the name of "*araṇi.*" By rubbing two pieces of this sacred wood together, the *brāhmaṇas* would ignite the fire for their sacrifices. It is very difficult to find and, therefore, not easily available. The *agni-hotri-brāhmaṇa* had some of this sacred *araṇi* wood tied to a churning stick, which he used to churn butter. Suddenly, a great deer grabbed the churning stick and fled with it, causing the *brāhmaṇa* great distress. "How can I continue my vow to do *havana* (offerings of ghee to the fire)?" he cried. He tried to catch the deer, but was unsuccessful. He became more and more distraught, as he knew it would be very difficult to find more of the sacred *araṇi* wood.

At that time, he heard that Yudhiṣṭhira Mahārāja, Bhīma, Arjuna, Nakula and Sahadeva had recently set their holy footprints in Dvaitavana. When he heard this, he became more hopeful about his situation. "Bhīma and Arjuna are very powerful fighters," he thought. "It is nothing for them to catch a deer. They are very submissive to their elder brother, Yudhiṣṭhira Mahārāja. If I submit a prayer to Yudhiṣṭhira Mahārāja, and he directs his younger brothers, then they will surely come to my aid and assist me in maintaining my religious vow of performing oblations."

He went to see the Pāṇḍavas. When he arrived, Yudhiṣṭhira Mahārāja and all the Pāṇḍavas stood up out of respect. The king, cordially receiving him, asked, "How can we serve you?"

The *brāhmaṇa* replied, "I am an *agni-hotri-brāhmaṇa*. I am to perform *havana* every day. But I have a problem. The sacred *araṇi* wood, used to ignite the fire for the oblations, was stolen by a deer. I tried to catch hold of the deer, but it was to no avail. You have with you the very powerful and formidable Bhīma and Arjuna. If you direct them, they will surely go to catch this deer and retrieve the sacred wood. In doing so, they will rescue me from the peril of the contravention of my religious vow—they will save me!"

Yudhiṣṭhira Mahārāja immediately directed his brothers to go and help this *brāhmaṇa*. They searched throughout the whole forest. Finally, toward the evening, they saw the deer, but could not catch it. Arjuna shot swarms of arrows into the sky, but was unsuccessful in catching the deer.

Disappointed, they returned and expressed their mental worries and agonies. They said to Yudhiṣṭhira Mahārāja, "We have never been unsuccessful before. We have lost all of our power! This is no doubt due to the fact that, when Duḥśāsana was trying to denude Draupadī in the assembly of kings, we did nothing to obstruct him. We have committed a great sin and have lost our power!"

Yudhiṣṭhira Mahārāja told them, "For now, we have other concerns. We are all very thirsty. Go through the forest and search for some drinking water. If there is no drinking water here, we shall all die."

Nakula, one of the younger brothers, climbed a tall tree and saw that, some distance away, there was a big lake. Yudhiṣṭhira Mahārāja directed Nakula to go search out that lake to find drinking water. When Nakula arrived there, he saw a very grand lake—very beautiful. Never before had he seen such a lake, with very pure crystal-clear water. Elegant swans swam in the lake while gardens of lotus flowers floated on top of the water. The sweet fragrance of the lotuses filled his nostrils. He was astounded to see this.

Nakula was very thirsty. He bent down to drink the clear water, when he suddenly heard a celestial voice, prohibiting him from drinking the water.

"Do not touch the water!" the voice said. "First you must answer my queries. If I receive appropriate answers from you, only then will you be permitted to drink the water! If you ignore me and touch that water, you will die!"

Nakula was so thirsty that he could not heed the request of that supernatural voice. He touched the water and immediately died.

Meanwhile, Yudhiṣṭhira Mahārāja was becoming worried that Nakula had not yet returned. He sent Sahadeva to investigate what had happened. When Sahadeva arrived at the lake, he was shocked to see his brother dead. But in his extreme thirst, he leaned down to touch the water and, just like Nakula, he heard a supernatural voice prohibiting him from doing so. But, like his brother, Sahadeva could not resist tasting the water. The instant he touched the water, he died.

After that, Yudhiṣṭhira Mahārāja sent Arjuna. On seeing his two brothers dead, Arjuna was deeply shocked. He went to the lake to take water for his elder brothers, when the voice called out to him, "Do not venture to touch the water! First give me answers to my queries, and then you may touch. Otherwise, you will also die!"

Arjuna searched for the source of the voice. Who was preventing him? Who was there? He searched, but saw nobody. He shot many arrows into the heavens, turning the sky dark.

Then, the voice addressed him once again, "You cannot shoot me with your arrows! You cannot stop me. First, answer my questions and then you may drink the water. Otherwise, you will suffer the same plight as your brothers."

"No!" Arjuna said. "I cannot remain here. My elder brothers are thirsty. I have to bring them water. After I bring them water, I shall come back."

Arjuna touched the water and also died.

After that, Bhīma was sent, who also died in the same fashion.

Ultimately, Yudhiṣṭhira Mahārāja, being very worried, came himself to the lake. When he saw that all of his four brothers were dead, he was grief-stricken. His intense grief is described for several pages in *Mahābhārata*. He thought, "This Duryodhana, Duḥśāsana, Karṇa and Śakuni are all hostile to the Pāṇḍavas. They are always trying to kill my brothers. Perhaps they have poisoned this lake and, by drinking this water, my brothers have died."

In his grief-stricken state, he saw the body of his brother Bhīma and lamented, "O Bhīma! You have taken the vow that you will split the thigh of Duryodhana! Now, how will you fulfill your vow?"

Yudhiṣṭhira Mahārāja wept.

Seeing the body of his brother, Arjuna, Yudhiṣṭhira Mahārāja called out to him, "O Arjuna! You are like Indra! There is no warrior equal to you. This is your fate? What shall I do?"

After a little while, he suddenly thought, "This water is very clean. It does not appear to have any poison in it. There are so many ducks and swans swimming about in it. There are also tortoises and fish. If this water were poisoned, then all these creatures would also die."

Yudhiṣṭhira Mahārāja looked at the bodies of his brothers. The four Pāṇḍavas looked as though they were sleeping. There were no wounds on their bodies, no deformities of any sort. "This is strange," the king thought. "It is as if they were in a deep slumber."

The king entered the lake and bathed. After he came out from his dip, he attempted to take a drink of the water.

He heard a supernatural voice saying, "I am a heron—a crane—a fish-eater! I am the owner of this lake. First, give answers to my queries. If you give me the appropriate answers, all your brothers will be brought back to life and you will also be permitted to drink the water."

Yudhiṣṭhira Mahārāja protested, "I do not believe that a heron can kill like a demon! How can a water bird kill a formidable soldier like Arjuna?"

Then the crane assumed the form of a palm tree, very tall with a black complexion. "I am a Yakṣa!" he exclaimed. "I have killed your brothers!"

The king was astounded.

The demon said, "First, give me the answers to my queries!"

Yudhiṣṭhira Mahārāja was, by nature, both sublime and sober.

He told the demon, "Yes, I shall try to give answers to your queries."

In *Mahābhārata*, we read that the crane demon asked many queries of Yudhiṣṭhira Mahārāja, but the last four questions are especially important.

kā ca vārtā kimāścaryaṁ
kaśca modate kaha panthāha
mamaitāṁścaturaha praśnān
kathayitvā jalaṁ piba
(Mahābhārata, Vana-parva 313.114)

Those queries were:
What is the news of the world?
What is the greatest wonder?
What is the true path?
Who is happy in this world?

To these questions, Yudhiṣṭhira Mahārāja gave answers that can never be changed. No person in the world can change these answers.

If someone were to ask us, "What is the news of the world?" we would reply, "Such-and-such things are happening in such-in-such place. There is a war somewhere or another, etc." After one month, everything would be completely changed. But Yudhiṣṭhira Mahārāja's answer to this question is immutable—it can never change. What is the verse in the *Mahābhārata*?

māsartudarvīparighaṭaṭnena
sūryāgninā rātridivendhanena
asmina mahāmohamaye kaṭāhe
bhūtāni pacatīti kālaha vārtā
(Mahābhārata, Vana-parva 313.118)

What is the meaning of this verse? "*Māsartudarvīparighaṭaṭnena*": the twelve months and six seasons are like spoons used for cooking. These months and seasons are rotating like the stirring of those spoons.

"*Sūryāgninā*": For cooking, fire is necessary. What is that fire? The sun.

"*Rātridivendhanena*": Where there is fire, there must be fuel. Fuel is consumed by fire. So, what is that fuel? The day and the night. When the sun rises, the day begins. When it sets, the night begins. Day and night are coming and going, so they are like fuel that is consumed by the sun.

There must be a pot for cooking—a large pot, a cauldron. What is the meaning of the cauldron? "Cauldron" means "*mahāmoha*"—great ignorance. We are in nescience. All the *jīvās*, being enveloped by the illusory energy of the Supreme Lord, believe that they are the masters and enjoyers of the world. They think, "This house is mine. This wife is mine. These children are mine. I am a *brāhmaṇa*, I am a *kṣatriya*, I am a *vaiśya*, I am a *śūdra*, I am an outcaste, I am Indian, I am Russian, I am American. This property belongs to me! I am the owner of this house." Actually, we are not the proprietors of anything. We belong to the Supreme Lord, and everything belongs to Him. By the influence of the illusory energy, we think that we belong to this world and that the things of this world belong to us. "I am of this world, I am Indian, I am Chinese, etc." This is false ego, false knowledge, the result of nescience. This is a big cauldron of illusion.

What are the articles to be cooked in this cauldron? The articles are the living beings. They will be cooked in that cauldron. So, who is the cook? Yamarāja, the god of death! He is cooking all the living beings of the world. Can anybody change this? Can anybody change this answer of Yudhiṣṭhira Mahārāja? Nobody can. When a cauldron is put over a fire, it will become very hot. If the living beings are thrown into that cauldron, they will feel its intense heat. All the living beings are afflicted with miseries. This is the news of the world! This is the whole picture. Nobody can change this answer.

The next question was, "What is the greatest wonder?" In our boyhood, in school, we were always taught that there were "seven wonders of the world." The Taj Mahal of Agra! In Babylon, there was a garden in the sky! In China, a gigantic wall! In Russia, a gigantic bell! In Egypt, the great pyramids, etc. But these are not wonders now. But the answer Yudhiṣṭhira Mahārāja gave to this question posed by Yamarāja cannot be changed by anyone. It is the answer for all time to come. What is this answer?

ahanyahani bhūtāni
gacchantīha yamālayam
śeṣāḥ sthāvaram icchanti
kim āścaryam ataḥ param
(Mahābhārata, Vana-parva 313.116)

Every day we are seeing that living beings are entering the jaws of death. Is it not so? Those who are younger than I, those who are older than I, those who are the same age as I, are all dying. But, those who presently exist are thinking that they will exist in this world this permanently. They are busy erecting huge buildings and other things thinking, "We shall remain here eternally!" Is this not a wonder? We think that we shall remain in this world eternally, even though we are seeing daily that all living beings are dying, regardless of their age. So, how is it possible that I will be able to remain in this world? Is this not the greatest wonder? Can anybody change this answer for all time to come?

The third question was, "What is the true path?" We are desperate to know what is the actual path of life. The answer to this question was given by Yudhiṣṭhira Mahārāja for all time to come, not to be disputed by anyone:

tarko 'pratiṣṭhaḥ śrutayo vibhinnā
nāsau ṛṣir yasya matam na bhinnam
dharmasya tattvaṁ nihitam guhāyāṁ
mahājano yena gataḥ sa panthāḥ
(Mahābhārata, Vana-parva 313.117)

Remember that this evidence is being given from *Mahābhārata*, not from any other scripture. *Mahābhārata* is accepted by all schools of thought in India. "*Tarka*": by the words of logical argument, you cannot substantiate any view or any contention. One intelligent person will establish one viewpoint, and another intelligent person, perhaps more intelligent, will refute that view and establish his own. Then a third person may come along and do the same. There is no foundation for this *tarka*, this reasoning, this mundane system of argument. In Bengal, it is said, "*viśvase mile vastu, tarke bahudūra.*" "By faith, we can get Bhagavān—by firm faith." Those who are without faith cannot get the Supreme Lord by means of bandy arguments and pedantic quips. "*Tarko 'pratiṣṭhaḥ.*" "*Śrutayo vibhinnā*": In the Vedas, you will find different kinds of teachings, because the status of each human being is different. There are three primary qualities of the Lord's external potency, *sattvas, rajas* and *tamas.* So, the human beings are enveloped by these qualities of the external potency of the Lord. If *sattva-guṇa* predominates, that person is called *sāttvika,* if *rajo-guṇa* predominates, that person is called *rājasika,* if *tamo-guṇa* predominates, that person is called *tāmasika.* So, each person has his own status:

trai-guṇya-viṣayā vedā
nistrai-guṇyo bhavārjuna
nirdvandvo nitya-sattva-stho
niryoga-kṣema ātmavān
(Bhagavad-gītā, 2.45)

In the *Vedas*, you will find different teachings for the *sāttvika* people, the *rājasika* people and the *tāmasika* people. But there are also teachings about the Transcendental Reality. That is also there. The *Vedas* are not like the Koran or the Bible. You cannot complete them in one lifetime. You may go through the *Vedas*—you may read thousands of verses—but you will still be unable to know what the actual teaching of the *Vedas* is. It is so vast. It is very difficult. According to the competence or worthiness of people, different kinds of teachings have been given for their gradual progress. So, it is very difficult to determine what the actual teaching of the *Vedas* is. "*Śrutayo vibhinnā nāsau ṛṣir yasya matam na bhinnam.*" "A *ṛṣi*, a saint, cannot be considered a saint if he does not have his own view." He will not be accepted as a saint:

"What is your view?"

"I've got no view."

"No! You are not a saint!"

Many minds, many views.

So, as we said earlier, people become confused and ask, "There are many saints. They all have different views. Which view should we accept? What is the path?" "*Dharmasya tattvaṁ nihitam guhāyāṁ, mahājano yena gataḥ sa panthāḥ*": "The concept of religion—spirituality—is concealed in the cave of a mountain." What is the meaning of this? "*Nihitam guhāyāṁ.*" "*Guhā*" means cave—a cave in the hills or mountains. "The religious concept is hidden in the cave of a mountain." "*Guhā*" means the cave of the heart of the surrendered soul, the *śuddha bhakta*. There have been many philosophical discussions on this topic among different philosophical groups in India. According to the theistic group, *dharmasya tattvaṁ*, the *tattva*—the thing in its true form—cannot be known by the human being by means of his own intellect or mental capacity. Why do they say this? If you claim that Ultimate Reality is that which can be perceived by human intellect and mental capacity, how correct can this be? The human being is born, he will remain for some time and then he will die. A human being is finite. His intellect is finite. His mental capacity is finite. Therefore, anything determined by means of human intellect and mental capacity will also be finite. How can he determine the infinite—the cause of himself or the cause of all things? How? Anything determined by the finite intellect or the finite mental capacity of the finite being will be a mentally concocted thing. That is not reality—it is fictitious. If reality is reality, it must always exist. Reality cannot be manufactured in the intellectual factory of the human being, a conditioned soul. That would be non-reality. Reality always exists. You are not to manufacture it by means of your limited mental capacity. Reality is there, and you have to find out how to see that truth. So, we say "*darśana-śāstra.*" The terms "*darśana-śāstra*" and "philosophy" are not synonymous. Nor are the terms "*dharma*" and "religion." There are many words in *sanātana-dharma* that are very peculiar. You cannot translate them into any language of this world. The word "philosophy" means "philo-sophia:" "love of knowledge." To which kind of knowledge is it referring? Empiric knowledge—knowledge acquired by the material senses and material intellect. Philosophy means that, depending on the data supplied by the senses and intellect, and utilizing the process of induction, one tries to ascertain Ultimate Reality. But you, yourself, are not an eternally existing person. You have been born and you will die. You have limitations. You are not the cause—you are the effect. So, you cannot determine your cause. That Cause is Self-effulgent. *Darśana-śāstra* means that truth is there, and you have to find the way to see that truth. You are not to manufacture *Bhagavān*. That which is manufactured is not reality. *Bhagavān* is there, and you have to find out how to see Him—*darśana-śāstra*. Unchallengeable Truth, the Cause of all causes, Who is Self-Effulgent and Self-Luminous, can descend to the completely surrendered soul. That complete submission is like a cave. God descends into the cave of the heart of the completely surrendered soul. Actual religion, or true righteousness, resides within the Supreme Lord, Supreme Reality. That Supreme Reality is the Absolute Conscious Person and, by His grace, He will reveal Himself to the submissive, surrendered soul.

You will find in *Śrīmad-Bhāgavatam*, that Brahmā, the creator of all living beings of this world, could not understand Kṛṣṇa. He was bewildered to see Kṛṣṇa. "This is a cowherd boy, how can he be Bhagavān?" he thought. But when he took complete shelter of the Lotus Feet of Nandanandana Śrī Kṛṣṇa, then he could understand. Only by Kṛṣṇa's grace could he understand. Brahmā, the creator of all the living beings of this world, could not understand by means of his own intellect and mental capacity. If we receive Kṛṣṇa's grace, we may take absolute shelter, but if we approach Him in a challenging mood, we will be disappointed. There is nothing greater than Him and nothing equal to Him, so without His grace, no one can know Him. If anyone says that he can know Him by his own means, then those means will be equal to, or greater than, Bhagavān. This is absurd. There can be no equal or superior to the Supreme Lord. Without His grace, nobody can know Him—it is the only way.

nāyam ātmā pravacanena labhyo
na medhayā na bahunā śrutena
yam evaiva vṛṇute tena labhyas
tasyaiva ātmā vivṛṇute tanuṁ svam
(Kaṭhopaniṣad, 2.23)

Paramātmā cannot be known by oration, lectures, intellect or education. Simply by being an "intellectual giant," a man cannot know Kṛṣṇa. Simply by being a great "Paṇḍita," possessing great knowledge of the scriptures, a man cannot know Kṛṣṇa. God will manifest His true form to those who surrender to Him.

Yudhiṣṭhira Mahārāja said, "*Mahājano yena gataḥ sa panthāḥ.*" The common definition of a Mahājana in India is a moneylender. So, a moneylender is very rich and generally has immense amounts of money that he can lend to others. But this is the ordinary meaning. Why do we actually earn money? To get happiness? Let us say that you are offered two proposals. The first proposal is that you will be a multi-millionaire, but you will always be in great suffering with many worries and tribulations. The other proposal is that you will always be very happy and never have any worries, but you will never have a farthing. Which proposal will you accept? Everybody wants happiness. We earn money for happiness—not for money's sake.

So, where can we find actual happiness? Kṛṣṇa is happiness personified.

Parents have great love for their small child. They find him very beautiful. "This beautiful child is making us so happy," they think. But then, perhaps, life leaves the body of that child. His body is dead, devoid of consciousness. If that dead body were preserved for a long time by means of a chemical procedure, could the body of that child give happiness to any father or mother? Of course not. Happiness belongs to consciousness—*cetana*. As long as *cetana* dwells within the cages of the physical and subtle bodies, the presence of that blissful entity is what gives us happiness. If an emancipated soul can come in contact with another person, that person can receive immense *ānanda*.

You will find in the autobiography of Aurobinda, that he was once a prisoner in a tiny cell. He says, "I felt suffocated from being in that cell. I felt that I should just die." But while he had these thoughts, he noticed some ants moving across the floor of his cell. He meditated upon this. By dint of his meditation, he concluded that within each ant there is a spiritual spark. Behind that, there is the All-Pervading Spirit. After meditating in this way, he felt some kind of solace. Material things cannot give us happiness. People, who cannot find anyone to be with them, might keep a dog or cat with them to keep them happy. We see that, sometimes, when a son or daughter leaves home, parents will bring some sort of pet into the home. Material things cannot make us happy. Some sort of sentient being must be there.

So, if a particle of a sentient being can give us so much happiness, then what can be said of the Cause of that tiny sentient being? Wherefrom are these sentient beings coming? Man can beget man. Horse can beget horse. Dog can beget dog. *Cetana* can beget *cetana*. We are all sentient beings. We have come from the Absolute Conscious Principle:

yato vā imāni bhūtāni jāyante
yena jātāni jīvanti yat
prayantyabhisaṁviśanti
tad vijijñāsasva tad brahma
(Taittirīya Upaniṣad 3.1.1)

We are emanating from Brahman, we are sustained by Brahman and we shall go to Brahman. That Brahman, as a conscious unit, is a person. But, we say that He is not a person: "That person is a myth, because he has no consciousness. No personality is attributed to this." But, personality is attributed to a conscious principle, not an unconscious principle. So, if an individual sentient being, possessing personal attributes, constitutes a person, then the Absolute Consciousness must also be a person—a personal being. "*Raso vai saḥ.*"

You will find that, in Kṛṣṇa-līlā, Yaśodā tried to fasten Gopāla, a small boy. A small boy, with a small belly. She took a length of rope to tie around His belly, but could not fasten it. All the ropes of Nanda Mahārāja, one after the other, forming a giant rope—from here to the airport—could not reach around the belly of Gopāla.

This is because within this "limitation", the small appearance of Gopāla, He is unlimited. "*Simār mājhe asīma tumi*" (saying by Ravindra Nātha Tagore).

Outwardly, we perceive Kṛṣṇa to have limitations but, within, He is actually unlimited. He is the Cause of all causes. He is inconceivable. We cannot understand this. Vast and infinite! That *Ānanda* can take any shape. *Ānanda* is transcendental and omniscient. Without His grace, you cannot get Him. If you can get Kṛṣṇa, you will be happy. There will be no end to it—it is infinite. Nobody can say, "I have tasted Kṛṣṇa!" After tasting again and again, his taste for Kṛṣṇa will still remain. But you are in this world. You might hear a very beautiful song, a very nice song. But after hearing it several times, it becomes stale and you yearn to hear a new song. But, within Kṛṣṇa's Name and Attributes, at every step you will find a new, fresh taste. You cannot end it. If you can enter into that region, then you will enter into the happiest region—the region of *kṛṣṇa-prema*. You will find, in *Śrīmad-Bhāgavatam*, the Mahājana is that person who is giving this knowledge of *kṛṣṇa-bhakti*. Who is a Mahājana?

svayambhūr nāradaḥ śambhuḥ
kumāraḥ kapilo manuḥ
prahlādo janako bhīṣmo
balir vaiyāsakir vayam

dvādaśaite vijānīmo
dharmaṁ bhāgavataṁ bhaṭāḥ
guhyaṁ viśuddhaṁ durbodhaṁ
yaṁ jñātvāmṛtam aśnute
(Śrīmad Bhāgavatam, 6.3.20-1)

Twelve Mahājanas are mentioned. Brahmā, Nārada, Rudra, the four Kumāras, Kapiladeva, Svayambhuva Manu, Prahalāda, Janaka

Mahārāja, Bhīṣma, Bali Mahārāja, Śukadeva Gosvāmī and Yamarāja are all Mahājanas. Here, Yamarāja is speaking to his messengers, the Yamadūtas. He says, "We twelve Mahājanas know *bhāgavata-dharma*. It cannot be understood easily, without the grace of Śrī Kṛṣṇa and His devotees. It is very confidential, most secret." So, those Mahājanas have advised us to love the Supreme Lord, Śrī Kṛṣṇa. If you love your country, such as the USA, then you will have to fight with other countries, such as those in Europe, Asia, etc. If you love the world, then you will be compelled to exploit *Maṅgala-graha* (the planet Mars). If you love this *brahmāṇḍa* (this material universe), you will try to exploit another *brahmāṇḍa*. But, if you love the Supreme, Complete Reality, you will have no impetus to exploit any other thing. So, this is the most elevated state—love of Complete Reality, the Supreme Lord.

The crane demon's final question was: "Who is happy in this world?" Yudhiṣṭhira Mahārāja replied:

pancamehāni ṣaṣṭhe vā śākaṁ pacātī sve gṛhe
anuṇī cāpravāsī ca sa vāricara modate
(Mahābhārata, Vana-parva 313.115)

At the end of the day, if a man takes only a little bread and nothing else, but has no debts and has not been forced to leave the land of his birth, then that man is happy. If anyone is in debt or cannot live in the place of his birth, then he is unhappy. This is an allegory, of course. The real meaning is this: We are *ātmā*. We are an eternally existing principle, *saccidānanda*. Therefore, if we have attachment to non-eternal things, that is known as "debt." We experience suffering proportionate to what we have spent in our involvement with non-eternal things. By the mercy of the *sādhu*, referred to here as a Mahājana ("money lender"), we shall become free from our debts. Because we are in debt, we have been driven from our home. Where is our home? "Back home, back to Godhead": That transcendental realm of Goloka is where we belong. We have been driven out to a foreign land, this material world. Whether we are in India, the USA or Russia, it is all foreign land. It is not our home. Our home is there in the transcendental realm. Therefore, we are suffering because we have been driven out from our actual birthplace, Goloka-Vṛndāvana, due to our attachment to these non-eternal things. This is the actual purport of the answer given by Yudhiṣṭhira Mahārāja.

After the crane demon, who was actually Dharmarāja (Yamarāja, the lord of death) in disguise, had heard all these answers from the king, he said, "Your answers are very good! One of your brothers may be brought back to life! Choose one only!"

Yudhiṣṭhira Mahārāja did not reveal his own feelings, but humbly requested that Yamarāja give back the life of his youngest brother Nakula. Yudhiṣṭhira was the son of Queen Kuntī and Nakula was the son of Queen Mādrī. Therefore, out of affection, he wished that each mother would have one surviving son, even though he was dependent upon the valor and strength of Arjuna and Bhīma for success in the inevitable war to come. Hearing this, Yamarāja said, "Actually, you are a righteous person. I shall bring all four of your brothers back to life! Then, you may request another boon from me."

Yudhiṣṭhira Mahārāja explained how the *agni-hotri brāhmaṇa* had lost his sacred wood to a deer. He requested Yamarāja to arrange to have it returned to him. To Yudhiṣṭhira Mahārāja's surprise, Yamarāja revealed himself once more. "I was that deer!" he said. "I myself took the wood. I shall return it to the *brāhmaṇa*. Is there some other wish that you desire?"

Yudhiṣṭhira Mahārāja then requested the boon that no one would be able to recognize them when the time came for the Pāṇḍavas to travel about incognito for one year at the end of their exile in the forest.

The Message of Bhagavad-gītā

Today's subject is "The Message of *Bhagavad-gītā*". You must have heard the name "*Gītā.*" It is universally adored. Everybody knows it. But the difficulty is this: there are thousands of commentaries on the *Gītā*, and in these commentaries the commentators have expressed their own views. They all have different views and ordinary people are confused about the actual message of *Śrīmad Bhagavad-gītā.*

The speaker of the *Gītā* is the Supreme Lord, Śrī Kṛṣṇa. Only those who have entered into the heart of Śrī Kṛṣṇa can understand the real implication and significance of His sayings and the purpose of His speech and advice. Outside people cannot understand.

But in India, and also outside India, you will find many people who say, "We do not believe Kṛṣṇa is the Supreme Lord because He took birth and, therefore, he was a human being. He may have many powers, perhaps even superhuman powers. He may even be a great politician, a great diplomat. But he is still only a human being."

Even those who have gone through the *Gītā* may also speak like this. It is most astounding. When I ask them, "Have you gone through the *Gītā*?" the reply is, "Oh, yes." I ask them, "How? If you have gone through the *Gītā*, then you should accept the teachings of the *Gītā.*"

Supreme Lord Śrī Kṛṣṇa says in the *Gītā*:

mattaḥ parataraṁ nānyat
kiñcid asti dhanañjaya
mayi sarvam idaṁ protaṁ
sūtre maṇi-gaṇā iva
(Bhagavad-gītā, 7.7)

"There is nothing superior to Me (*mattaḥ*)." With emphasis, Śrī Kṛṣṇa says that He is the Supreme Lord. We read the *Gītā*, but we do not believe the teachings of Supreme Lord Śrī Kṛṣṇa. Why is this? "*Mattaḥ parataraṁ nānyat, kiñcid asti dhanañjaya, mayi sarvam idaṁ protaṁ, sūtre maṇi-gaṇā iva*": "Nothing is separate from Me. Everything exists inseparably within Me, just as gems are inseparable when strung on a thread."

ahaṁ hi sarva-yajñānāṁ
bhoktā ca prabhur eva ca
na tu mām abhijānanti
tattvenātaś cyavanti te
(Bhagavad-gītā, 9.24)

"I am the only Master and the only Enjoyer of all *yajñās* (sacrifices)." "*Ahaṁ*": "I am the only one." "*Ahaṁ hi*": "Certainly, surely I am." "I" denotes a person. "*Na tu mām abhijānanti tattvenātaś cyavanti te*": "Those who do not believe this are detached from reality."

There are many other *ślokas* in the *Gītā* substantiating Śrī Kṛṣṇa as the Supreme Lord:

ahaṁ sarvasya prabhavo
mattaḥ sarvaṁ pravartate
iti matvā bhajante māṁ
budhā bhāva samanvitāḥ
(Bhagavad-gītā, 10.8)

"I am the cause of all creation, the origin of all things." "*Ahaṁ*": "I" and "*mattaḥ*": "from Me" do not signify an impersonal God. Kṛṣṇa says to Arjuna, "*Sarvam pravartate*": "All are set into action by My initiative and imparted power."

brahmaṇo hi pratiṣṭhāham
amṛtasyāvyayasya ca
śāśvatasya ca dharmasya
sukhasyaikāntikasya ca
(Bhagavad-gītā, 14.27)

"*Brahmaṇo hi pratiṣṭhāham*": "I am the cause of the impersonal, formless God (Brahman)." That impersonal, formless God is the halo of Śrī Kṛṣṇa's own light, emanating from Śrī Kṛṣṇa Himself. *Pratiṣṭhā* means "foundation." Śrī Kṛṣṇa is the foundation of Brahman. "*Amṛtasyāvyayasya ca*": He is the foundation of *amṛta* (ambrosia), the foundation of *avyaya* (imperishability) and the foundation of *śāśvata* (eternity). He is also the object of *vraja-prema*, one-pointed pure love and devotion, as exemplified by the inhabitants of Vraja-dhāma.

Kṛṣṇa is the Supreme Lord. How can we know the Supreme Lord? Without His grace, no one can know Him. If anybody says, "Yes, I can know Him," then he will be equal to or greater than the Supreme Lord. But the Supreme Lord, Infinite and Absolute, is One. Nothing can be outside the Infinite. If you say, "This flower is outside the Infinite," then the Infinite becomes finite. Even a particle of dust cannot be outside the Infinite, or the Absolute will lose His position. The Absolute is One. The only way to get Him is to take absolute shelter at His Lotus Feet and to act according to His will. There is no other way to get Him except by means of exclusive, pure devotion.

Therefore, only those who have surrendered to Śrī Kṛṣṇa, who have access to the heart of Śrī Kṛṣṇa, can understand the implication and significance of His teachings. Those without knowledge of Śrī Kṛṣṇa, who have not submitted to Śrī Kṛṣṇa, how can they know? They may write many commentaries, but they cannot comprehend the actual significance of the teachings of Śrī Kṛṣṇa.

Seeing the sad plight of the conditioned souls of this world, the Supreme Lord, Śrī Caitanya Mahāprabhu, out of compassion, sent His own men—Śrīla Bhaktivinode Ṭhākura and Śrīla Bhaktisiddhānta Sarasvatī Gosvāmī Ṭhākura—to the world to rescue the fallen souls. Śrīla Sarasvatī Gosvāmī Ṭhākura, through his entourage, extended His grace all over the world. They were very powerful spiritual personalities. They refuted all anti-devotional contentions by means of sound reasoning and scriptural evidence. Bhaktivinode Ṭhākura has written his commentary on the significance of the teachings of the *Gītā*. If we go through his writings, we shall come to know the real implication of the teachings of the *Gītā*.

Śrī Saṅkarācārya has written this glorification at the end of the *Gītā*:

gītā su-gītā kartavyā
kim anyaiḥ śāstra-vistaraiḥ
yā svayaṁ padmanābhasya
mukha-padmād-viniḥsṛtā
(Śrī Saṅkarācārya's Gītā-māhātmyam, 4)

"The *Gītā* should be rightly read with one-pointed devotion, for the satisfaction of Śrī Kṛṣṇa. No other scripture is necessary if one takes shelter of the *Gītā*. The *Gītā* emerges from the holy lips of Śrī Kṛṣṇa and is one with Him." It is not material sound. In material sound, you will find that the thing referred to by a sound is different from the sound itself. If you utter: "water, water, water," the water-word is not the water-thing. The word "water" refers to a thing understood to be water. In this world you will find a difference between the word "water" and the object referred to by the word "water." But Kṛṣṇa and the Name of Kṛṣṇa are one and the same. *Gītā* and Kṛṣṇa are identical. So, by taking shelter of the *Gītā* we can come in contact with Kṛṣṇa. We have gone through the contents of the *Gītā*, we have read the *Gītā*, but despite this, we still have no devotion to Kṛṣṇa. This is not actual reading. If we actually read the *Gītā*, we will obtain devotion to Śrī Kṛṣṇa.

As I have stated earlier, without the grace of Śrī Kṛṣṇa, we cannot know the significance of the teachings of the *Gītā*. Lord Caitanya Mahāprabhu has instructed us on this point. During His visit to South India, He encountered a *brāhmaṇa* at the Raṅganātha Temple who used to read the *Gītā* daily with great devotion. The *brāhmaṇa* had no knowledge of Sanskrit. As such, he committed mistakes in pronunciation. Many pandits (religious scholars) also used to visit the temple. When they heard this *brāhmaṇa* reading the *Gītā* and committing mistakes, they objected thus:

"Why are you reading the *Gītā*? First, you should learn Sanskrit. Learn to pronounce Sanskrit correctly, then read it."

But, he did not pay heed to any of the remarks made by these people and, with rapt attention, he would read the *Gītā* from beginning to end. Eventually, Lord Caitanya Mahāprabhu came to visit the Raṅganātha Temple and saw the *brāhmaṇa* reading the *Gītā* with great concentration and devotion. Lord Caitanya Mahāprabhu was greatly attracted by this *brāhmaṇa*. He stood at the back of the temple, listening attentively. After completing his reading of the *Gītā*, the *brāhmaṇa* stood up and saw Śrī Caitanya Mahāprabhu, the Extraordinary Divine Personality, Who was tall, with arms down to His knees and a golden complexion. Lord Śrī Caitanya Mahāprabhu expressed His satisfaction, "I am very glad to hear your recitation of the *Gītā*."

The *brāhmaṇa* said, "I have no right to read the *Gītā*, but it is the order of my divine master. He said, 'You should read the *Gītā* completely, from beginning to end, and only after that may you take any food.' I cannot understand any of the verses because I have no knowledge of Sanskrit."

Lord Caitanya Mahāprabhu said, "You say that you do not

understand the *Gītā*, but while you were reading the *Gītā* you were weeping. Tears were flowing from your eyes—why? If you did not understand the *Gītā*, why were you weeping?"

The *brāhmaṇa* replied, "I have never divulged my heart to anyone, but You are a divine personality. It is not good to conceal my heart before You. It is true, I do not understand the *Gītā*, but while I read the *Gītā*, I see before me the Supreme Lord, Śrī Kṛṣṇa working as a servant, having been subdued by the devotion of Arjuna. He is the Supreme Lord, the Lord of all lords, the Lord of infinite *brahmāṇdas* and infinite *vaikuṇṭhas*. Seeing His Bhakta-Vātsalya Mūrti (His form of profound affection for His devotee), I cannot control the flow of tears from my eyes. It happens spontaneously. It is very surprising that the Supreme Lord is working as a driver and His devotee is giving Him orders!"

senayor ubhayor madhye
rathaṁ sthāpaya me 'cyuta
(Bhagavad-gītā, 1.21)

Arjuna said to Kṛṣṇa, "O Acyuta, place my chariot in front of the armed forces of the rival warring factions."

Lord Caitanya Mahāprabhu said to the *brāhmaṇa* with great assertion, "Your reading of the *Gītā* is crowned with success, as you have devotion to Śrī Kṛṣṇa."

Many people have distorted the teachings of the *Gītā* to fulfill a vile mentality. Once, a younger godbrother of our Guru Mahārāja, Pūjyapāda Bhakti Kumud Śānta Gosvāmi Mahārāja, went to Kashmir during the time of the British administration. At that time, the Mahārāja of Kashmir was Hari Siṁha. He arranged a meeting, including Svāmījī as one of the royal guests. The invitees were all dignitaries, rich people, and many of them owned tea gardens. The Mahārāja of Kashmir also owned tea gardens. Our *śikṣā* guru,

Pūjyapāda Śānta Mahārāja, is a very spirited person. He does not hesitate to tell the truth. In His speech, he said emphatically, "Those who are virtuous should not commit sins. They should not gamble, they should not engage in illicit connections with women, they should not slaughter animals and they should not take intoxicants of any kind, including even tea."

The tea garden owners were thunderstruck upon hearing this. They thought that they had committed a mistake by inviting Svāmījī and said, "We are advertising tea, and Svāmījī has come to destroy our business!"

One of the tea garden owners came to Svāmījī and said, " Svāmījī! You have spoken against tea, but it is glorified in the *Gītā*."

Svāmījī said, "I have gone through the *Gītā* several times. I have not seen it."

"Yes, it is there."

In India the word for "tea" is "*ca* (pronounced 'cha')." The tea garden owner showed Śānta Mahārāja a specific verse from the *Gītā*:

sarvasya cāhaṁ hṛdi sanniviṣṭo
mattaḥ smṛtir jñānam apohanaṁ ca
vedaiś ca sarvair aham eva vedyo
vedānta-kṛd veda-vid eva cāham
(Bhagavad-gītā, 15.15)

"In the form of "*ca*", 'tea', I have entered into the heart of every *jīvā* (living entity). And lastly, Kṛṣṇa Himself says 'I am *ca*' (*cāham*), meaning, 'I am tea'."

This is certainly not the meaning. The meaning has been twisted here to serve an ulterior motive. This sort of commentary will misguide the reader and be of no benefit. In the Sanskrit language, the word "*ca*" means "and", not "tea" as it does in Hindi. The real meaning of this verse is, "I reside in the heart of every living being as the Indwelling God. The living being's memory and knowledge, previous precepts and concepts as well as forgetfulness of these things, have all come from Me. All the *Vedas* substantiate Me as the only object to be known. I am the author of the *Vedānta (vedānta-kṛd)*, and I am versed in the *Vedas* (*veda-vid*)."

The *Gītā* is part of the *Mahābhārata*. Vaiśampāyana Ṛṣī narrated the infatuation and mourning of Arjuna to Janmejaya in the Bhīṣma-parva of the *Mahābhārata*. Sañjaya obtained a boon from Vyāsadeva Muni that he would be able to see the events unfolding at the site of the battle of Kurukṣetra, so as to narrate the same to Dhṛtarāṣṭra:

dhṛtarāṣṭra uvāca
dharma-kṣetre kuru-kṣetre
samavetā yuyutsavaḥ
māmakāḥ pāṇḍavāś caiva
kim akurvata sañjaya
(Bhagavad-gītā, 1.1)

Dhṛtarāṣṭra asked Sañjaya, "My sons, Duryodhana and others, the Pāṇḍavas, Yudhiṣṭhira Mahārāja and others, assembled in the holy place of Kurukṣetra with the desire to wage war. What did they do?"

Viśvanātha Cakravartī has said in his commentary: "They have come with the desire to fight—they will fight. This much is unquestionable. But Dhṛtarāṣṭra had some doubt about this: 'Kurukṣetra is a holy place, and the Pāṇḍavas are naturally religious-minded. They will accept an agreement or treaty but my sons may not accept. However, by the influence of Kurukṣetra, their minds may change, so there may be a peace agreement.' That doubt was in Dhṛtarāṣṭra's mind, so he asked Sañjaya what they did. But inwardly, he was thinking, 'If there is no war, then our sons will be in danger from the Pāṇḍavas throughout their lives. So it is better that there should be a fight'."

As per the desire of Arjuna, Kṛṣṇa placed the chariot before the Kauravas (the army led by Dhṛtarāṣṭra's sons). Shivering, Arjuna was bewildered to see all his relatives before him. He saw in front of him his paternal grandfather, Bhīṣma, his guru Droṇācārya, as well as his paternal uncles, brothers-in-law, kith and kin. He became perplexed. He thought, "All have come to sacrifice their lives. If I win the kingdom by killing them, I shall not be happy. Let them kill me, I shall not fight." He set aside his legendary, powerful bow, Gāṇḍīva.
Upon seeing the infatuation of Arjuna and his reluctance to fight, Śrī Kṛṣṇa reproached him, saying:

kutas tvā kaśmalam idaṁ
viṣame samupasthitam
anārya-juṣṭam asvargyam
akīrti-karam arjuna
(Bhagavad-gītā, 2.2)

"O Arjuna! How have you become so infatuated at this most critical juncture in front of the hostile opponents on the battlefield? This may be befitting to a non-Aryan, but this sort of deliberation of yours at this stage is unwarranted. This will deter you from attaining celestial prosperity and will also destroy your name and fame."

klaibyaṁ mā sma gamaḥ pārtha
naitat tvayy upapadyate
kṣudraṁ hṛdaya-daurbalyaṁ
tyaktvottiṣṭha parantapa
(Bhagavad-gītā, 2.3)

"O Pārtha (son of Pṛthā, or Kuntī-devī)! You should not become impotent. It does not befit you. Shake off your weakness of heart, rise up and be ready to fight. You are capable of crushing the enemy."

aśocyān anvaśocas tvaṁ
prajñā-vādāṁś ca bhāṣase
gatāsūn agatāsūṁś ca
nānuśocanti paṇḍitāḥ
(Bhagavad-gītā, 2.11)

"You are speaking to me as though you were a very learned person, but you are mourning for that which is undeserved. The wise do not mourn either for those who are born or for those who are dead, because *ātmā* (the real self) is eternal, having no birth or death."

dehino 'smin yathā dehe
kaumāraṁ yauvanaṁ jarā
tathā dehāntara-prāptir
dhīras tatra na muhyati
(Bhagavad-gītā, 2.13)

"A corporeal living entity undergoes transformations of his body—childhood, youth and infirmity. Death is also a kind of transformation. The wise do not become deluded by this."

na jāyate mriyate vā kadācin
nāyaṁ bhūtvā bhavitā vā na bhūyaḥ
ajo nityaḥ śāśvato 'yam purāṇo
na hanyate hanyamāne śarīre
(Bhagavad-gītā, 2.20)

"*Jīvātmā* has no birth and no death. He is not reborn and experiences no growth. He is unborn and eternal. He always exists in the past, present and future. He is ancient but always fresh. When the body is killed, *ātmā* is not slain."

mayaivaite nihatāḥ pūrvam eva
nimitta-mātraṁ bhava savya-sācin
(Bhagavad-gītā, 11.33)

"O Savyasācin (O Ambidextrous One—Arjuna, who is expert in shooting arrows with the left hand), I have already killed everyone. You are only an instrument in this. Shake off the false conception that you are the killer."

Then Arjuna thought, "I spoke about virtue, but Śrī Kṛṣṇa is dissatisfied. He has reproached me. Perhaps I am wrong in my discernment of truth and falsehood."

kārpaṇya-doṣopahata-svabhāvaḥ
pṛcchāmi tvāṁ dharma-sammūḍha-cetāḥ
yac chreyaḥ syān niścitaṁ brūhi tan me
śiṣyas te 'haṁ śādhi māṁ tvāṁ prapannam
(Bhagavad-gītā, 2.7)

Arjuna said, "I have lost my natural valor. I am bewildered and cannot ascertain what is right and what is wrong. I submit to you. I am your disciple. Please advise me regarding my eternal welfare."

Arjuna had taken shelter at the Lotus Feet of the Supreme Lord. Then, Kṛṣṇa, acting as Guru, began to advise Arjuna and, via Arjuna, all the conditioned souls of the world. Śrī Kṛṣṇa gave various instructions in the *Gītā* befitting the competency or ability of individual souls. He gave advice about *karma* (the path of performing correct action), *jñāna* (the path of knowledge), *yoga* (the path of austerity and meditation) and *bhakti* (the path of pure devotion). But if we go through the *Gītā* thoroughly and carefully, we will find that, ultimately, Kṛṣṇa takes all to *bhakti* (devotion).

Kṛṣṇa first extols the virtues of *karma* and inspires everyone to engage in it:

na hi kaścit kṣaṇam api
jātu tiṣṭhaty akarma-kṛt
(Bhagavad-gītā, 3.5)

"No one can remain without *karma* (action) for even a moment."

niyataṁ kuru karma tvaṁ
karma jyāyo hy akarmaṇaḥ
śarīra-yātrāpi ca te
na prasiddhyed akarmaṇaḥ
(Bhagavad-gītā, 3.8)

"Always perform *karma* (i.e., *nityā-karma*, or eternal *karma*, as enjoined in the scriptures). Doing *karma* (performing one's duty) is better than not doing *karma* (not performing one's duty), as no one can sustain his or her body without *karma* (work or action). There are three kinds of *karma*: *karma*, *akarma* and *vikarma*. *Karma* is the performance of actions or duties enjoined by the Vedas, *akarma* is abstinence from actions or duties enjoined by the Vedas and *vikarma* is the performance of actions or duties prohibited by the Vedas. Actual doers of *karma* in the world are very rare. Kṛṣṇa has recommended *karma* but, ultimately, He is taking us to *bhakti:*

yajñārthāt karmaṇo 'nyatra
loko 'yaṁ karma-bandhanaḥ
tad-arthaṁ karma kaunteya
mukta-saṅgaḥ samācara
(Bhagavad-gītā, 3.9)

"Perform *karma* for *Yajña.*" "*Yajña vai viṣṇurti śrute.*" In *śruti śāstra*, Viṣṇu is described as *Yajña* and one of His names is *Yajña.* "*Yad idaṁ viśvaṁ vyapnotiti viṣṇuḥ*": "Viṣṇu is the all-pervading Supreme Lord,

Complete Reality." If we perform any action for the Supreme Lord, Complete Reality (*pūrṇa*), we will not fall into bondage. If we perform action for any part, separate from the Whole, we will fall into bondage. "*Oṁ tat sat.*" The Supreme Lord is *tat*, transcendental: that which cannot be comprehended by gross and subtle material senses.

We should perform actions for the Supreme Lord without any desire for the fruits of the actions. To perform any action for the Supreme Lord is *bhakti*, devotion. By inspiring a person to do *karma*, Kṛṣṇa takes the *karmī* (the doer) to *bhakti*.

When Śrī Kṛṣṇa speaks about *jñāna*, He extols it thusly:

na hi jñānena sadṛśaṁ
pavitram iha vidyate
tat svayaṁ yoga-saṁsiddhaḥ
kālenātmani vindati
(Bhagavad-gītā, 4.38)

"There is nothing so sanctified as *jñāna.*"

yathaidhāṁsi samiddho 'gnir
bhasma-sāt kurute 'rjuna
jñānāgniḥ sarva karmāṇi
bhasma-sāt kurute tathā
(Bhagavad-gītā, 4.37)

"As a blazing fire burns wood, reducing it to ashes, so too does *jñāna* destroy all kinds of *karma,* reducing it to ashes." *Karma* is initiated by the false ego of the doer.

prakṛteḥ kriyamāṇāni
guṇaiḥ karmāṇi sarvaśaḥ
ahaṅkāra-vimūḍhātmā

kartāham iti manyate
(Bhagavad-gītā, 3.27)

"The *jīvās*, being enveloped by the illusory energy of the Supreme Lord, which consists of three primal qualities or *guṇas* (*sattvas:* goodness, *rajas:* passion and *tamas*: ignorance), misunderstand these qualities to be the body and wrongly think themselves to be the doers." When *sattva-guṇa* predominates, we become *sāttvika*; if *rajo-guṇa* predominates, *rājasika*; and if *tamo-guṇa* predominates, *tāmasika*. As per the color of the false ego, *karma* is also of three colors (white, red and black).

The *jñānīs* (those who practice the path of knowledge) strive for self-realization. So all *karma* (deluded activity) emerging from the material ego is destroyed by *jñāna* (proper knowledge). But by recommending *jñāna*, Kṛṣṇa is ultimately taking us to *bhakti*.

bahūnāṁ janmanām ante
jñānavān māṁ pradadyate
vāsudevaḥ sarvam iti
sa mahātmā su-durlabhaḥ
(Bhagavad-gītā, 7.19)

"After many births, the proponents of *jñāna-mārga* (the path of knowledge) take absolute shelter of Me (Vāsudeva). Such a saint who sees everything in relation to Vāsudeva is rarely to be found."

When their knowledge has reached the stage of maturity, *jñānīs* can understand that no one can know God without His grace. As there is no one equal to or greater than Śrī Kṛṣṇa, no one can attain Him without His grace.

Śrī Kṛṣṇa, Himself, has pronounced a comparative judgment in regard to this in the *Gītā*:

tapasvibhyo 'dhiko yogī
jñānibhyo 'pi mato 'dhikaḥ
karmibhyaś cādhiko yogī
tasmād yogī bhavārjuna

yoginām api sarveṣāṁ
mad-gatenāntar-ātmanā
śraddhāvān bhajate yo māṁ
sa me yuktatamo mataḥ
(Bhagavad-gītā, 6.46-47)

"O Arjuna! Become a *yogī*, as a *yogī* is superior to a hermit who practices severe austerities. The *yogī* (the worshipper of Paramātmā) is superior to the *jñānī* (the worshipper of formless Brahman), and is naturally, supremely superior to the *karmī* (one who performs actions enjoined by the scriptures for mundane benefit). Among all kinds of *yogīs*, one who, while concentrating his mind on Me, worships Me (My Eternal, Transcendental Form) with firm faith and devotion is the highest *yogī*. Hence, the *bhakti-yogī* is the highest among *yogīs*."

yasmāt kṣaram atīto 'ham
akṣarād api cottamaḥ
ato 'smi loke vede ca
prathitaḥ puruṣottamaḥ
(Bhagavad-gītā, 15.18)

"As I am beyond *kṣara* (the individual soul) and am supremely superior to *akṣara* (Brahman and Paramātmā), I am renowned in this world as Puruṣottama, the Supreme Personality. This is corroborated by all the *Vedas*."

Arjuna had certainly been listening to Kṛṣṇa's instructions, yet

Kṛṣṇa now says, "Hear Me" ("*śṛṇu me*"). Śrī Kṛṣṇa wanted to emphasize that Arjuna should pay special attention to His next pronouncement:

sarva-guhyatamaṁ bhūyaḥ
śṛṇu me paramaṁ vacaḥ
iṣṭo 'si me dṛḍham iti
tato vakṣyāmi te hitam
(Bhagavad-gītā, 18.64)

"O Arjuna, even if you have been unmindful of my instructions thus far, it will not be so detrimental to you, but you should hear Me now with great care and attention. As you are My most beloved, I am telling you this topmost secret of all secrets, My supreme commandment, for your eternal welfare."

This is the highest instruction that Śrī Kṛṣṇa has given to all the conditioned souls of the world for their eternal welfare via Arjuna:

man-manā bhava mad-bhakto
mad-yājī māṁ namaskuru
mām evaiṣyasi satyaṁ te
pratijāne priyo 'si me
(Bhagavad-gītā, 18.65)

"Devote your mind to Me. If it is difficult to devote your mind to Me, just serve Me—engage your senses in My service. If this is also not possible, just worship Me. If even that is not possible, then take absolute shelter of Me. I promise you, surely, you will attain Me."

In spite of this, Arjuna was oscillating and could not decide what to do. Therefore, Kṛṣṇa gave these final directions:

sarva-dharmān parityajya
mām ekaṁ śaraṇaṁ vraja

ahaṁ tvāṁ sarva-pāpebhyo
mokṣayiṣyāmi mā śucaḥ
(Bhagavad-gītā, 18.66)

"Relinquish all My previous spiritual instructions about *dharma* (the relative duties of *varṇa* and *āśrama* as enjoined by the *Vedas*) and take absolute shelter of Me. I shall rescue you from all sins. Do not be overwhelmed by grief."

According to the *Gītā* (7.4-5), the physical, gross body (composed of earth, water, fire, air and sky) and the subtle body (composed of mind, intelligence and perverted ego) are the outcome of the *aparā* potency (inferior material energy) of Supreme Lord Śrī Kṛṣṇa. The real self, *ātmā*, is the outcome of the *parā* potency (superior spiritual energy) of the Supreme Lord. Body, mind and *ātmā* all belong to Supreme Lord Śrī Kṛṣṇa. It is the duty of all individual spirit souls to serve Kṛṣṇa.

Arjuna said:

naṣṭo mohaḥ smṛtir labdhā
tvat-prasādān mayācyuta
sthito 'smi gata-sandehaḥ
kariṣye vacanaṁ tava
(Bhagavad-gītā, 18.73)

"O Acyuta, by Your grace my bewilderment has now been removed. I have remembered that I am Your servant, and all my doubts have been dispelled. I have come to learn that submission to You is the eternal, highest function of each and every individual soul. I shall do whatever You order me to do!"

And then the fight begins. But Arjuna's fight is for devotion!

The Significance of Ekādaśī-vrata

Today is a most auspicious day: Mohinī Ekādaśī. Ekādaśī means "*hari-vāsara*." This *tithi* (day of the lunar month), the bright moon fortnight Śukla Ekādaśī, is very dear to Lord Hari. In one word: *hari-vāsara*. For this reason, it is most auspicious. This is its specialty. So if you perform *bhajana*, worship of Kṛṣṇa, by means of *śravaṇaṁ*, *kīrtanaṁ*, *smaraṇaṁ* (hearing, chanting and remembering) and other devotional forms on Ekādaśī, you will get a million times more benefit than on other days. If you realize the utility or benefit of following this vow then you will be actuated to observe it.

There are two kinds of benefit. In the *sanātana-dharma* scriptures of India there are two main divisions, *karma-kāṇḍa* and *bhakti*. *Karma-kāṇḍa* is the part of the Vedic literatures that prescribes rituals and ceremonies suitable for the obtainment of material, temporary benefits. This is called *karma-kāṇḍa—smārta*. From *smṛti* comes the word *smārta*. Those *brāhmaṇas* who are well versed in *smṛti* are called *smārta-brāhmaṇas*. They prescribe laws and regulations taken from the *smārta* scriptures advising, "If you perform this sort of vow you will get this sort of benefit." To encourage worldly people, they speak of worldly benefits. By this, the worldly-minded are inspired, but pure devotees do not want any such material, temporary benefits. This is called *śuddha bhakti* (pure devotion). One is the *śuddha bhakti* line and the other is the *smārta* line. They are quite different.

Now, in the scriptures you will find a description of the glory and utility of observing Mohinī Ekādaśī. This description can be found in the *Sūrya Purāṇa*, which is named after the sun god, Sūrya. What is the nature of this glory, utility or benefit? Yudhiṣṭhira Mahārāja asked Supreme Lord Śrī Kṛṣṇa, "Kindly tell me what the name of the Ekādaśī is, in the bright moon fortnight of the month of Vaisakha (April/May), and what benefit will we get by observing this Ekādaśī? Please tell me." Kṛṣṇa replied, "I will not respond to your question based upon my own initiative," that is to say, based upon His own opinion. That is the procedure. You will find that even the Supreme Lord and the sages observe this procedure of presenting evidence based upon the previous evidence given by self-realized souls.

Śrī Kṛṣṇa continued, "Vasiṣṭha Muni played the pastime of acting as the guru of Bhagavān Rāmacandra. Bhagavān Rāmacandra once put a specific question to His guru. "I am experiencing extreme grief caused by separation from My consort, Sītā Devī. Why is this happening to Me? How can I overcome this extreme separation grief?" Vasiṣṭha Muni replied, "You are the Supreme Lord. By uttering Your Name everyone will be emancipated and delivered from all kinds of difficulties, so why are You questioning me like this? You are surely putting this question to me for the benefit of the enslaved *jīvās* of this world, who have the desire to obtain their eternal welfare. You are asking on behalf of those who strive diligently toward this goal. To obey Your order, I say that if You observe the Mohinī Ekādaśī *vrata*, it will destroy all sins, even heinous ones. If You observe this vow, You will be relieved of Your separation grief. I shall provide an example to illustrate this point."

Vasiṣṭha Muni continued, "There was a city, a metropolis, called Bhadravatī, on the bank of the river Sarasvatī, that was the capital of the kingdom, and in this city resided a king by the name of Dyutimana. This king was very religious-minded, righteous and pious. In that kingdom, there was also a *vaiśya* by the name of Dhanapāla. *Vaiśya* indicates the third social class, the business class. They engage in business as the means of earning their livelihood and are often quite wealthy. This person, like the king, was very pious. He always acted for the benefit of humanity and for the good of all, including the subjects of the king. Everyone was very grateful and respectful toward him. He had five sons, but it was his misfortune that his youngest son, Dhṛṣṭabuddhi, was without good character—a debauchee. Dhanapāla was, naturally, very disappointed with the situation. He thought, "What is this? My son is squandering the money that I collect and he is also associating with prostitutes. He is committing all kinds of heinous crimes."

One day, Dhanapāla saw his youngest son walking along the road while embracing the neck of a harlot. At the sight of this, he was very much distressed and disappointed. He thought, "I don't want this son. I'll drive him out. He should go. I don't like his behavior." Dhanapāla then drove his son out from his home.

Due to the prestigious social position and wealth of his father, Dhṛṣṭabuddhi had some money with him for several days after being driven out. However, when this money ran out, he had to resort to all kinds of criminal activity, such as robbery, eventually leading to his arrest by the police. When the police realized that he was the son of the respected Dhanapāla, they released him. Ultimately, he had no choice but to live in the dense forest where he killed the beasts and birds for sustenance. He was committing all kinds of sins. Otherwise, how would he survive with no money? All of a sudden, he saw coming toward him, in wet clothing, a great saint by the name of Kauṇḍinya Muni, who had just finished bathing. Upon encountering him, a drop of water fell from the *muni's* wet clothing onto Dhṛṣṭabuddhi and he was immediately sanctified. Dhṛṣṭabuddhi became repentant, thinking to himself, "I have spoiled my whole life. I have deprived myself of the affection of my parents. What have I done?" Thinking in this way, he fell down at the feet of Kauṇḍinya Muni saying, "Please rescue me. You are all-merciful. Please rescue me, as I am the most wretched creature. There is no soul more fallen than I." In this way, he repeatedly offered prayers to Kauṇḍinya Muni, who was compassionate by nature. Kauṇḍinya Muni said, "Who are you?" Dhṛṣṭabuddhi introduced himself, informing Kauṇḍinya Muni of his unfortunate plight. Kauṇḍinya Muni then told him not to worry and advised, "If you observe Mohinī Ekādaśī, all your previous sins will be destroyed. It is the scriptural prescript and law to observe this vow." Accordingly, Dhṛṣṭabuddhi followed his advice and he was relieved of the burden of all his sins. Not only this, but he went to the Lotus Feet of the Supreme Lord by observing Ekādaśī.

In the *karma-kāṇḍa śāstra* you will find that this sort of encouragement is being given, but the *śuddha bhaktas* observe Ekādaśī solely for the satisfaction of Śrī Kṛṣṇa. What is the real purpose of Ekādaśī? Our *smṛti-grantha,* or Vaiṣṇava *smṛti* book, is called *Hari-Bhakti-Vilāsa*. In this, there are laws or rules stipulating how to properly perform all the vows that have devotion to the Supreme Lord as their goal. Those who are pure devotees like to act in accordance with the injunctions of the devotional literatures, especially *Hari-Bhakti-Vilāsa*. In this literature, the actual purpose of observing Ekādaśī is written:

upāvṛttasya pāpebhyo
yas tu vāso gunaiḥ saha
upavāsaḥ sa vijñeyaḥ
sarva bhoga vivarjitaḥ
(Śrī Hari-Bhakti-Vilāsa, 13.14)

"Giving up all sins, and with all good qualities, one who remains near Kṛṣṇa, totally relinquishing all enjoyments, has actually observed the vow of Ekādaśī." *Upāvṛttasya pāpebhyaḥ*: We are to give up all sinful activity. We are to refrain, to desist from committing all sins. On Ekādaśī-tithi this is the very least we should do and, while exhibiting all good qualities, we should remain near the Supreme Lord Who is All-Good, All-Existence, All-Knowledge and All-Bliss. *Upavāsa*. *Upa* means near to, in the vicinity of, or in the proximity of. *Vāsa* means to remain, to remain near God. It is generally thought that *upavāsa* means to remain without food, to fast. If you remain without food, but you think to yourself, "When shall I eat? My stomach is burning with hunger," then you are not thinking about Kṛṣṇa. You are thinking about your stomach. If that should be the case, then you can take food that is allowed by the scriptures, but you should always think about Kṛṣṇa.

āpo mūlam phalam payaḥ
havir brāhmaṇa kāmyā ca
guror vacanam auṣadham'e
aṣṭaitānyavrataghnani
(Śrī Hari-Bhakti-Vilāsa, 12.40, quoted from the
Udyoga-parva of Mahābhārata)

If you take the foods stated in this verse, there will be no breach of your vow. You can take water. *Mūlam* means potatoes and other roots that grow under the earth. You can boil them and your vow will not be broken. *Phalam*—all kinds of fruits can be taken. Cow's milk and milk preparations such as yogurt and ghee (clarified butter) can also be taken. With ghee from cow's milk, you can prepare a curry from vegetables like potatoes or other roots. Green bananas (plantains) and papaya are also acceptable. There will also be no breach of vow if medicine is taken which doctors have prescribed for a serious, possibly life threatening, health problem. If a bonafide *brāhmaṇa* would like to take something, then he or she should fulfill their desire in such a way that their vow will not be destroyed. However, one should take note that the actual prescript of the devotional scriptures is that, on Ekādaśī, one should always remain near Bhagavān—all day and night. We should not forget Him. There are many prohibitions, many commandments, both positive and negative assertions. There is a list of things that one should not do, a list of negative assertions. Should there be any kind of action that will make you forget Kṛṣṇa, then that is also prohibited even if it is not included in the list. There are also commandments, nine forms of devotion, sixty-four forms of devotion—like this. Should there be any other kind of action or devotion that will remind you of Kṛṣṇa or the service of Kṛṣṇa, then that is allowed even though it may not be on the list. What is the criterion to understand what we are to do and what we are not to do?

smartavyaḥ satataṁ viṣṇur
visamartavyo na jātucit
sarve vidhi-niṣedāḥ syur
etayor eva kiṅkarāḥ
(*Padma Purāṇa, quoted in Caitanya Caritāmṛta, Madhya-līlā 22.113*)

We have to remember Kṛṣṇa always. That is the prescript or injunction of the devotional scriptures. We should never forget Him. So, therefore, the purpose of observing this vow of Ekādaśī is to remember Kṛṣṇa always. Wherever your mind is, you are there also. You are here now in this temple but you are thinking about your house and your relatives, who may be there experiencing difficulty of some sort. Or, perhaps, you are thinking that there is some work at home that requires your attention. If you are thinking like this, then where are you actually staying? You are physically staying here at the temple, but mentally you are staying at your house. Is it not so? Wherever your mind rests, wherever your mind remains, you will be there also. If you go to Vṛndāvana but you do not think about Vṛndāvana, then where are you staying? Physically you are there, but mentally you are somewhere else. The primary factor is the mind. In all the different devotional forms of worship, the target is to engage the mind in the service of Kṛṣṇa. If you can control the mind all the senses will be controlled automatically as they are subservient to the mind. "*Sarve mano nigraha lakṣṇāntam.*"

Now the difficulty is this: *sarva bhoga vivarjitaḥ*. On this day, you have to give up all kinds of *bhoga*, sensuous enjoyment. Totally! If you have the inclination to enjoy, you can only enjoy that which is inferior to you. You will not be able to remain near Viṣṇu, Bhagavān or the *bhakta* because They are superior. If you have the spirit of enjoyment you will remain near material things, the temporary, non-eternal things of this world—things that you can lord it over. If you want to observe Ekādaśī, to remain always near Kṛṣṇa, then you have to give up all kinds of enjoyment totally. You have to remain near Kṛṣṇa, but there is yet another problem. What is that problem? Who is Kṛṣṇa? Kṛṣṇa is not a human being:

harir hi nirguṇaḥ sākṣāt puruṣaḥ prakṛteḥ paraḥ
(*Śrīmad-Bhāgavatam, 10.88.5*)

Hari (Kṛṣṇa) is transcendental. He is beyond mind, intelligence and the sense organs of the conditioned souls of this world. You cannot stay near Hari by means of this physical body composed of earth, water, fire, air, ether and the astral body, composed of mind, intellect and perverted ego, which are produced by the *aparā* potency of Supreme Lord Śrī Kṛṣṇa (the material energy). An example can be given. The owner of a building is residing on the tenth floor and his servant is residing on the ground floor of that building. If the servant stays on the ground floor, will he be able to serve the owner of the building? He must go upstairs to the tenth floor by means of walking or by taking the elevator and he must enter the apartment and then the room where the owner may be lying down. He must then proceed to the bedstead where he can sit and give a massage if necessary. By remaining on the ground floor, he cannot serve. Similarly, the Supreme Lord is in the transcendental realm but you are on the mundane plane, with this physical body. How, then, are we to remain near the Supreme Lord? Tell me. Does the Supreme Lord have a material form?

īśvaraḥ paramaḥ kṛṣṇaḥ
sac-cid-ānanda-vigrahaḥ
anādir ādir govindaḥ
sarva-kāraṇa kāraṇam
(Śrī Brahma-Saṁhitā, 5.1)

He is the Cause of all causes. He has *vigrahaḥ* (form) but it is made of *sat* (eternal existence), *cit* (knowledge) and *ānanda* (bliss), not of material things. How then, can I remain near Kṛṣṇa with this material body? The devotional, spiritual injunction is that we should remain near God. But God is transcendental, beyond our comprehension, so the problem is, how are we to stay near Him? What is the solution? We find in Śrī *Caitanya Caritāmṛta*:

dīkṣā-kāle bhakta kare ātma-samarpaṇa
sei-kāle kṛṣṇa tāre kare ātma-sama
sei deha kare tāra cid-ānanda-maya
aprākṛta-dehe taṅra caraṇa bhajaya
(Śrī Caitanya Caritāmṛta, Antya-līlā, 4.192-193)

"At the time of taking *mantra-dīkṣā*, the devotee takes absolute shelter of Gurudeva. Śrī Kṛṣṇa makes the devotee *cid-ānanda-māyā* via the medium of Gurudeva and, in that transcendental form, the devotee can worship Śrī Kṛṣṇa."

What is the significance of this? *Dīkṣā-kāle bhakta kare ātma-samarpaṇa*: *Dīkṣā* means *mantra-dīkṣā* and *harināma-dīkṣā*. There are two kinds of *dīkṣā* and when we take *dīkṣā*, we surrender to the Lotus Feet of Gurudeva and to the Lotus Feet of the Supreme Lord. However, we are not seeing the Supreme Lord. The Supreme Lord is here in His Deity form, but He is not talking with us. We cannot exchange thoughts with Him even though He is here in His Deity form. Very rarely, among many, many human beings, we may find a devotee of Kṛṣṇa to whom the *Mūrti* or Deity is speaking, but generally we experience no exchange of thoughts. On the other hand, although we know that the material body and the things related to it are temporary, we exchange thoughts with them and as a result we become attached. We have attachment for non-eternal, physical relations but we have no attachment for Kṛṣṇa. What can be done? What is the procedure? You will find in the dialogue between Kapila Bhagavān and Mātā Devahūti in the 3rd Canto of Śrīmad Bhāgavatam:

prasaṅgam ajaraṁ pāśam
ātmanaḥ kavayo viduḥ
sa eva sādhuṣu kṛto
mokṣa-dvāram apāvṛtam
(Śrīmad Bhāgavatam, 3.25.20)

You are seeing the *sādhu*. The *sādhu* is moving and talking. The real or bonafide *sādhu* has one-pointed devotion to Supreme Lord Śrī Kṛṣṇa. He is giving everything—mind, intelligence, speech and senses—everything, for the service of Kṛṣṇa. He is serving Kṛṣṇa twenty-four hours a day. Such a *śuddha bhakta* is rarely to be found. You should go to a *śuddha bhakta*, but who is a *śuddha bhakta*? Kapila Bhagavān says that a *śuddha bhakta* must have this original quality of one-pointed devotion to the Supreme Lord; otherwise he cannot be accepted as a *śuddha bhakta*. One should find a *śuddha bhakta* such as our Gurudeva, Śrīla Bhakti Dayita Mādhava Gosvāmī Mahārāja. By speaking with him and seeing his outward appearance, everyone was attracted. Some even thought that he was the son of Śrīla Bhaktisiddhānta Sarasvatī Ṭhākura due to their striking physical similarity. Of course, Śrīla Bhaktisiddhānta Sarasvatī Ṭhākura had no son, as he was an ascetic. For those who have not personally seen our Paramgurudeva, Śrīla Bhaktisiddhānta Sarasvatī Ṭhākura, it should be noted that he would think and speak about Kṛṣṇa twenty-four hours a day. Many pandits, erudite scholars, would come to debate with him, thinking to challenge his contentions and refute what he was preaching, but when they actually saw him, they would become speechless and bow down before him. So much power! They were astounded at the sight of him because his knowledge was not merely that of books, but of realization sent by Śrī Caitanya Mahāprabhu. It is a completely different thing.

Śrīla Bhaktisiddhānta Sarasvatī Ṭhākura was in the habit of sending our Gurudeva in advance to functions, as Śrīla Gurudeva was always very successful in his endeavors wherever he went. One such occasion was when our Paramgurudeva visited Sarabhoga, Assam for the first time. There was a great reception for Śrīla Prabhupāda when he arrived. While in Sarabhoga, Śrīla Bhaktisiddhānta Sarasvatī Ṭhākura traveled in a bullock cart while others walked to different places in the area. At that time, one of my senior godbrothers, Śrīla Āśrama Mahārāja, was a young *brāhmaṇa* boy acting as family guru there in Assam. While following Paramgurudeva's cart one day, the *brāhmaṇa* boy who was perhaps one or two years older than myself, asked Paramgurudeva what his name was and where he had come from. The resulting conversation destroyed his connection with family life. So therefore, conversing with a *sādhu* is very dangerous! By seeing, hearing and engaging in a dialogue with Śrīla Prabhupāda, the *brāhmaṇa* boy became very much attracted. His family had placed many restrictions upon him, such as you should not go outside, you should take mantra here, etc., but instead he renounced everything and he came to our Maṭha. The *śuddha bhakta* is so attractive! Upon first sight, Śrīla Āśrama Mahārāja was attracted. This boy had no prior knowledge of scripture but because the *śuddha bhakta* is gracious to all, being the grace incarnate of the Supreme Lord, he was attracted by only a brief encounter. The grace of the *śuddha bhakta* extends to all living beings, not just to human beings, because they are one with Kṛṣṇa. They are equal to all and they show affection to everyone and it is this affection that attracts people. Paramgurudeva was ordered by Śrīla Gaura Kiśora dāsa Bābājī and Śrīla Bhaktivinoda Ṭhākura to preach the message of Śrī Caitanya Mahāprabhu. The Pañcatattva appeared to him, telling him, "Do not be afraid. We are giving you this order." Within a very short time, he stirred the whole world. So many disciples came—our Gurudeva, Purī Gosvāmī Mahārāja, Bon Mahārāja, Bhaktivedanta Svāmī Mahārāja and Śrīdhara Mahārāja—all stalwart figures! In this way, he expanded himself. So, if you take shelter of the Lotus Feet of Gurudeva, who is the absolute counterpart of Śrī Bhagavān, Kṛṣṇa will accept you through that medium and make your body transcendental.

"*Dīkṣā-kāle bhakta kare ātma-samarpaṇa*": *Dīkṣā* does not merely mean hearing the mantra. It means submitting totally to the lotus feet of a bonafide guru. Kṛṣṇa gives His grace through the guru, who is grace incarnate. If you want to see the sun, you cannot do so by ignoring the light from the rays of the sun. First the light will come and, through the medium of that light, you will see the sun. The sun is self-effulgent, self-luminous. And in the night, if you want to see the sun, you will not be able to see it. Even if you connect all of the electric lights of the world, you will not be able see the sun at night. You might see the light of those electric lights and mistakenly think that this is the sun, but it is not. You have to wait for the sun to rise. When the sun rises, you have to accept the grace of the sun, you have to take the sun. You should not close your eyes—you have to open them. You have to open the doors and windows. You have to accept. Then, through that medium, you will see the sun. There is no other way. Self-effulgent God is the Cause of all causes. He has no cause, so He is Self-Evident Truth, Self-Luminous. By His grace, you can get Him. That grace-incarnate form is guru. If you are very fortunate, you can come in contact with the *sādhu*, the bonafide guru. God graces us all through the medium of the devotee. "*Dīkṣā-kāle bhakta kare ātma-samarpaṇa, sei-kāle kṛṣṇa tāre kare ātma-sama*": at the time when we sincerely submit to the bonafide guru, who is the grace incarnate of Supreme Lord Śrī Kṛṣṇa, through that medium, Śrī Kṛṣṇa will take us, He will embrace us, and make our body transcendental—fit for sitting near Him. "*Sei deha kare tāra cid-ānanda-maya, aprākṛta-dehe tañra caraṇa bhajaya*": that transcendental spiritual form can worship Kṛṣṇa. With this body, you cannot enter the transcendental realm of Vṛndāvana. Vṛndāvana is not a material part of India. It has descended. Gods descends, His realm descends and His associates also descend. Even Śrī Caitanya Gauḍīya Maṭha is not a part of Calcutta or Chandigarh. Śrī Caitanya Gauḍīya Maṭha has descended there. Where can you perform worship of Śrī Śrī Rādhā-Kṛṣṇa? Only in the transcendental realm, in Vṛndāvana-dhāma. Rādhā-Kṛṣṇa always remain in Vṛndāvana-dhāma. By the grace of a true devotee, one may receive the service of Rādhā-Kṛṣṇa. An ordinary person cannot perform this service. So, Vṛndāvana is not a part of the world, it is not a part of India, it is not a part of Uttar Pradesh. Vṛndāvana, the transcendental spiritual realm, has descended there. We must submit to Kṛṣṇa to understand.

In the 10th Canto of *Śrīmad Bhāgavatam*, Lord Brahmā, the creator of the material universe, stole the cowherd friends and calves from Śrī Kṛṣṇa, thinking Kṛṣṇa to be an ordinary boy. Lord Brahmā was bewildered by this form of Kṛṣṇa as a simple cowherd boy, thinking that, if Kṛṣṇa were Bhagavān, He would exhibit great opulence and majesty. Now the point is this: if Brahmā could not understand Kṛṣṇa, then how can we understand Him? It is very difficult. For this reason, when we take absolute shelter of Gurudeva, the grace incarnate of Śrī Kṛṣṇa, Kṛṣṇa will grace us and we will become competent to receive a form comprised of *saccidānanda*. In that form, we can remain near Kṛṣṇa and observe Ekādaśī correctly, but this is very difficult. It is not so easy. However, having said this, there is one easy way for the enslaved *jīvās*.

Caitanya Mahāprabhu, Himself, has taught us what we are to do on Ekādaśī. We are familiar with Nārada Muni in Kṛṣṇa-līlā. In Caitanya-līlā, Nārada appeared as Śrīvāsa in Māyāpura-dhāma to fulfill the pastimes of Gaurāṅga Mahāprabhu. In Śrīvāsāṅgana, the home of Śrīvāsa Paṇḍita, Caitanya Mahāprabhu used to perform *saṅkīrtana* along with His personal associates, Nityānanda Prabhu, Advaitācārya Prabhu, etc., throughout the whole night for an entire year, taking no sleep. If we remain sleepless for even one night, then we will have to go to the hospital for a week!

Now, what does Caitanya Mahāprabhu teach that we should do on Ekādaśī?

harivāsare, hari-kīrtana vidhāna
nṛtya ārambhila prabhu jagatera prāṇa
(Caitanya Bhāgavata, Madhya-līlā 8.138)

Śrī Vṛndāvana dāsa Thākura here describes the scene of Caitanya Mahāprabhu dancing and chanting at the house of Śrīvāsa Paṇḍita on Ekādaśī. The devotional prescripts are that you have to perform *kīrtana. Kīrtana-vidhāna.* You are to utter the Holy Name. That Name and the Named are identical. You cannot remain in the vicinity of the Deities when the Deities are asleep and the doors are closed. But you can utter the Name any time of day or night. Caitanya Mahāprabhu has said that He has imbued the Holy Name with a special power in this Kali-yuga:

nāmnām akāri bahudhā nija-sarva-śaktis
tatrārpitā niyamitaḥ smaraṇe na kālaḥ
etādṛśi tava kṛpā bhagavan mamāpi
durdaivam īdṛśam ihājani nānurāgaḥ
(Śrī Śikṣāṣṭaka 2)

We are unfortunate that we have no desire to utter the Holy Name. The Name and the Named are the same. So, you have to perform *harināma* always: "*hari-vāsara hari-kīrtana.*" To observe the vow of Ekādaśī correctly, you have to abide by the rules and regulations for eating, etc. That you should do. But the main thing is that you have to remain near Kṛṣṇa. You have to utter the Name. Because the Name and the Named are the same, when you utter "Kṛṣṇa," you will be near Him. Kṛṣṇa and the Name "Kṛṣṇa" are identical:

nāma cintāmaṇiḥ kṛṣṇaś
caitanya-rasa-vigrahaḥ
pūrṇaḥ śuddho nitya-mukto
'bhinnatvān nāma-nāminoḥ
(Śrī Bhakti-Rasāmṛta-Sindhu, Pūrva-vibhagaga 2.233,
quoted from Padma Purāṇa)

We are uttering all these evidences, so we should have belief! "*Nṛtya ārambhila prabhu jagatera prāṇa*": Caitanya Mahāprabhu started dancing. Who is Caitanya Mahāprabhu? He is the life of all the living beings of the world. He is the most beloved. You will find the following verse in the 7th Canto of *Śrīmad Bhāgavatam*, wherein Prahlāda is speaking to the demon boys:

na hy acyutaṁ prīnayato
bahv-āyāso 'surātmajāḥ
ātmatvāt sarva-bhūtanāṁ
siddhatvād iha sarvataḥ
(*Śrīmad Bhāgavatam 7.6.19*)

Prahlāda Mahārāja says, "It is not very difficult to satisfy Kṛṣṇa, because He is the Most Beloved Object of all the *jīvās*." You will find in this world that the mother is the most beloved of the child. But you will also see that there is some self-interest involved. In this world, without there being something that satisfies one's self-interest, you will not find any love. Nonetheless, we see that there is such a thing as affection between mother and child. Now, let us suppose a child is given a biscuit and, as he is eating it, that biscuit falls onto the ground. That biscuit, wet with the saliva of the child, will become covered with dust and other things on the ground. Then the child might give that biscuit to his mother, saying, "Here, eat this." The mother would not ordinarily eat such a thing, but to satisfy her child, she puts the biscuit to her mouth. So it is not very difficult to please Kṛṣṇa because He is the Most Beloved. You can chant, "Oh, Hari! Oh, Kṛṣṇa! Where are You? Please forgive me. Please bless me." If you can utter this from the core of your heart, then He will be pleased. You have nothing to give Him. He does not want anything: He has infinite wealth. You can attract Him only by your devotion. With sincere devotion, you can utter the Name. This is true under all circumstances.

punyavanta srivasangne shubhārambha
(Caitanya Bhāgavata, Madhya-līlā 8.139)

Śrīvāsāṅgana became the most sacred and holy of places by Śrī Caitanya Mahāprabhu's powerful *saṅkīrtana*. The most auspicious commencement had begun. What was that?

uthila kirtana dhvani
gopāla govinda
(Caitanya Bhāgavata, Madhya-līlā 8.139)

hari o' rāma rāma
hari o' rāma rāma
(Caitanya Bhāgavata, Madhya-līlā 23.92)

The utterance of the Name of Gopāla, Govinda—loud shouting of the Name of Govinda—had started. That sweet sound, that transcendental sound, you will not find in this material world. You have notes, tones, etc., in this world. But that transcendental sweet sound of the utterance of the Holy Name—"Gopāla! Govinda! Hari Rāma! Rāma! Hari Rāma! Rāma!"—will rescue us. You should do *harināma*. It is very easy. If you do *harināma*, you will be near Kṛṣṇa.

You will get more benefit on Ekādaśī if you perform your worship at a temple—a place where the devotees are assembled to worship the Supreme Lord. This is also called "*dhāma*." If you perform worship in the transcendental realm—in Mathurā-dhāma, Vraja-maṇḍala, Navadvīpa-dhāma or Puruṣottama-dhāma—you will get more benefit. Wherever devotees assemble and sing the glories of the Supreme Lord is also *dhāma*:

mad-bhaktā yatra gāyanti
tatra tiṣṭhāmi nārada
(Padma Purāṇa)

Kṛṣṇa was telling Nārada, "Where do I stay? Wherever my devotees sing the glories of My Name, Form, Attributes, Pastimes and Personal Associates is the place that I stay." So if you observe this practice in the company of bonafide *śuddha bhaktas*—*sādhus*—it will have special efficacy.

The effect of observing Ekādaśī is illustrated in the story of the life of Ambarīṣa Mahārāja. Ambarīṣa Mahārāja observed Ekādaśī tithi with great devotion in Mathurā-dhāma, Vraja-maṇḍala, for one year at a stretch. Kṛṣṇa was so satisfied by this, that the curse of Durvāsā Ṛṣi could not touch Ambarīṣa Mahārāja. In the 9th Canto of *Śrīmad Bhāgavatam* you will find that Śukadeva Gosvāmī spoke the following to Parīkṣit Mahārāja:

nāspṛśad brahma-śāpo 'pi
yaṁ na pratihataḥ kvacit
(Śrīmad Bhāgavatam, 9.4.13)

The curse of a *brāhmaṇa* cannot go unfulfilled or be warded off. But nonetheless, it could not touch Ambarīṣa Mahārāja. Parīkṣit Mahārāja was astounded to hear this. "I was born in the Pāṇḍava family. The Pāṇḍavas are very dear to Kṛṣṇa. When I was in the womb of my mother Uttarā, Aśvatthāmā threw a *brahmāstra*, a missile, with the aim of destroying all the Pāṇḍavas. At that time, when my mother was crying, Supreme Lord Śrī Kṛṣṇa protected me with His Sudarśana-cakra by covering my mother's womb. So my name is Viṣṇurāta, as I have been protected and saved by Viṣṇu. I was also able to see my Object of Worship, Śrī Kṛṣṇa, from within the womb. After my birth, I searched for that object, 'Where is that Purūṣa? Where is that Object of Worship?' I was examining. The Sanskrit word '*parīkṣa*' means, 'examining.' So, my name is Parīkṣit." He continued, "I was born in the Pāṇḍava family, I was protected by Kṛṣṇa. I also saw Kṛṣṇa when I was in the womb and after birth I tried to find that Purūṣa Whom I had seen. Yet I am waiting here, knowing that after seven days I shall be killed by snakebite, having been cursed by the son of Śamīka Muni."

The history of this curse began when, one day, Parīkṣit Mahārāja had gone to the cottage of Śamīka Muni to ask for water, as he was very thirsty. At that time, Śamīka Muni was meditating and was unconscious of Parīkṣit Mahārāja's presence. When he received no response, Parīkṣit Mahārāja became enraged, "I am in your cottage. You are not offering water to a thirsty person?" So, with indignation and wrath, he placed a dead snake around the neck of the *muni* as an insult. After Parīkṣit Mahārāja left the cottage and returned home, he repented, "Pāṇḍavas always respect *brāhmaṇas*, *munis*. I have been born in the Pāṇḍava family. I have done a very wrong thing." In this way, he deeply repented his behavior, and prayed to Supreme Lord Śrī Kṛṣṇa, "Oh, Śrī Kṛṣṇa, please punish me, as I have done a very wrong thing."

Outside the cottage of Śamīka Muni, his son, Śṛṅgi, had been playing with the sons of the other *ṛṣis*. When Śṛṅgi came to the cottage, he saw that someone had put the body of a dead snake around the neck of his father. He was disheartened and became furious. "Who has done this sinful thing? If I am the son of my father, a *brāhmaṇa*, then I curse that on the seventh day from today, the person who has done this will be killed by snakebite!" Then he began to weep.

Śamīka Muni opened his eyes. "What is the matter?" he asked. "Why are you weeping?"

Śṛṅgi said, "Somebody has insulted you with this dead snake." He told his father about the curse he had placed on whoever had done this.

Śamīka Muni said, "Oh! You have done the wrong thing. Parīkṣit Mahārāja is a religious minded person, born in the Pāṇḍava family. He has the right to chastise me. You are a *brāhmaṇa*, but you became impatient and have improperly delivered this curse."

Śamīka Muni sent a *ṛṣi* boy to the capital city of Parīkṣit Mahārāja to inform him of the curse, so that he could prepare himself for its effect. The boy reached the court of Parīkṣit Mahārāja and told him that the son of Śamīka Muni had cursed him to die by snakebite after seven days.

Then Parīkṣit Mahārāja became happy. "Yes," he thought. "Kṛṣṇa has love for me, so He has sent this curse giving me seven days time until I shall die. Nobody can know in advance that he will die at a specific moment. But I have been granted the time to prepare for seven days."

So, he made up his mind to renounce his household life. He called his son, Janamejaya, and told him, "You take over my position as king. I am going to Sukartāla by the side of the Ganges. I have no time to waste. I must prepare myself. You remain here."

At times of peril and danger, our minds become changed. I had one such experience when I was a college student. I was sent by our revered father to Victoria College in Coochbihar, where I received my Bachelor of Arts degree. There was a very big hostel there. Once, a famous astrologer came there and predicted that at such-and-such time, on such-and-such date, there will be universal dissolution. Everything will be annihilated—destroyed. All the residents of the hostel gathered together—I was among them—and they were saying that the prediction of this astrologer would come true, since he had never been wrong before. So, there we were, considering what we should do. We thought, "We shall die in the evening. Everything will be destroyed." There was a restaurant within the compound of the hostel. We all decided, "Let us eat! Let us go to the restaurant and eat as much as we can enjoy. Our parents have given us money, so let us utilize it. They will be very happy that we have the brains to reason that we shall all die, so what is the use of keeping this money? Let us go." I also went with them to the restaurant. Everyone was ordering various kinds of sweets from the waiter. We were eating and eating and eating and, after some time, we could not eat any more. We spent all our money, so we thought we were very intelligent. "Our parents will think that we have done well," we thought.

After that, we went to our room and discussed things until the time for the end of the world was to come. The time came and passed, and there was no dissolution, no end of the world, nothing. "Oh-ho! We have been deceived! What will we say to our parents?" We discussed this among ourselves.

During all this, one of our friends had been asleep in the room. All of a sudden, he woke up. He started shouting, "Universal dissolution!! Universal dissolution!!" He was crying and running about. He fell down, shouting. The people who saw him asked, "Where is the universal dissolution? What is he saying? He must have had a bad dream."

During all this, no one had suggested, "Let us worship Śrī Kṛṣṇa." I also had not said anything. I had gone along with them because there were so many of them. What could I say? They took me along. Like that, when there are no eternal good deeds, no eternal good impressions, no "*sukṛti*" (as it is called in scripture), nobody has the aptitude to worship Kṛṣṇa. Even if we are told, "In the evening, everything will be destroyed! You should prepare and worship Kṛṣṇa," we still will not worship Him. We will go off with the students, to enjoy.

Parīkṣit Mahārāja is a Vaiṣṇava. He made the decision to renounce his household life and, consequently, went to Śrīkanta. I have been to that place with Guru Mahārāja several times. It is in Uttar Pradesh, about 20 kilometers from Muzaffarnagar. It is still considered to be a sacred place. When Parīkṣit Mahārāja went there, all the *ṛṣi munis* also went there, thinking that something miraculous was about to happen, because Parīkṣit Mahārāja is no ordinary person. Then Parīkṣit Mahārāja asked them, "I have only one week's time. Please advise me what I should do." There were many *ṛṣis*—*karmi-ṛṣis, jñānī-ṛṣis,* and *yogī-ṛṣīs*—all offering different methods of obtaining emancipation.

Some of the more ordinary *karmi-ṛṣis* said, "You have money. If you donate money, then you will be rescued.

Others among the *karmi-ṛṣis* said, "No, there isn't much time. You have to perform oblations," and they gave him a list of articles that he should obtain so they could make sacrifices.

A third group, made up of *jñānī-ṛṣis* said, "No, no! By performing these *karma-kāṇḍa* sacrifices, you cannot be rescued. You have to perform meditation!"

The *yogī-ṛṣīs* insisted that he should perform *prāṇayāma*.

Parīkṣit Mahārāja was puzzled. "What should I do?" he thought. Then he took absolute shelter of the Lotus Feet of Supreme Lord Śrī Kṛṣṇa. "Please rescue me! I have a family connection with the Pāṇḍavas. Please show me the path!"

Then Kṛṣṇa sent His own man, Śukadeva Gosvāmī. You cannot automatically get the company of the bonafide *sādhu*. There must be some good qualities, some previous good impressions (*sukṛti*). Otherwise, you cannot get it. At that time, Śukadeva Gosvāmī was only sixteen years of age. He was *mahā-tyāgī*, completely renounced, and he wandered through the villages naked. All the villagers thought he was a mad person. They would throw stones and other things at him. Śukadeva Gosvāmī would not object to this, because he was beyond this world. The villagers could not understand Śukadeva Gosvāmī. But when he set his holy footprints in Sukartāla by the side of the Ganges, all the *ṛṣi-munis* stood up upon seeing him, out of respect. A learned person can give respect to a learned person. An ignorant person has no capacity to understand a learned person. A *sādhu* can understand a *sādhu*. A non-*sādhu* cannot understand a *sādhu*. All the *ṛṣi-munis* assembled there understood that he was not an ordinary man.

When Śukadeva Gosvāmī arrived there, he spoke to Parīkṣit Mahārāja. "I am Śukadeva. Before coming here, I was firmly established in *brahmānanda* but I have been attracted by the absolute, sweet qualities of Śrī Kṛṣṇa:

pariniṣṭhito 'pi nairguṇya
uttama-śloka-līlayā
gṛhīta-cetā rājarṣe
ākhyānaṁ yad adhītavān
(*Śrīmad Bhāgavatam*, 2.1.9)

So, I am advising you to hear about the Supreme Lord, Śrī Kṛṣṇa for these seven days. You should not do anything else."

No *ṛṣi-muni* had the capacity to say anything against this advice. They all sat there while Śukadeva Gosvāmī sang and narrated the glories of Supreme Lord Śrī Kṛṣṇa. Parīkṣit Mahārāja attentively listened for seven days without taking anything—without taking water, without taking food and without taking rest. Can we do this?

Śukadeva Gosvāmī was worried. "Mahārāja," he said, "Won't you take some rest? Perhaps a little bit of water or some food?"

Parīkṣit Mahārāja answered him, "You should not concern yourself with this. I have no time!"

naiṣātiduḥsahā kṣun māṁ
tyaktodam api bādhate
(Śrīmad Bhāgavatam, 10.1.13)

I am thirsty. I know that without water, nobody can survive. I am also hungry. But this hunger and thirst cannot become an obstacle to my hearing, because I have no time. After seven days I shall die. So, do not think about me. I have no feeling for these things. My mind is here:

pibantaṁ tvan-mukhāmbhoja-
cyutaṁ hari-kathāmṛtam
(Śrīmad Bhāgavatam 10.1.13 continued)

"You are distributing *hari-kathāmṛtam* and I so am satisfied. I have no thirst, no hunger. I do not require any rest."

Continuously, he heard for seven days and he attained the objective.

Nowadays if you assemble ten, twelve or perhaps one hundred persons under such conditions, everyone will be fidgeting with discomfort. But Parīkṣit Mahārāja maintained pin-drop silence.

So, Parīkṣit Mahārāja asked, "Even though I was born in the Pāṇḍava family and Kṛṣṇa has protected me, I am waiting here because after seven days I shall be killed. So, what then of Ambarīṣa Mahārāja and the curse of a *brāhmaṇa* like Durvāsā? Even if anyone hears about Durvāsā, they tremble because Durvāsā can remain without food for one thousand years. But, he can also eat one thousand years' worth of food in one day. So everyone shivers when they hear that he may be coming. 'He may bless us, or he may curse us!' they think. He is such a powerful *ṛṣi*, but his curse could not even touch Ambarīṣa Mahārāja? That is very astounding!" he exclaimed.

But, because Ambarīṣa Mahārāja had observed Ekādaśī, as per the devotional, scriptural injunctions, for one year, Kṛṣṇa was satisfied and the curse of Durvāsā Ṛṣi could not harm him.

Then, Parīkṣit Mahārāja wanted to hear the holy biography of Ambarīṣa Mahārāja. Śukadeva Gosvāmī said:

ambarīṣo mahā-bhāgaḥ
sapta-dvīpavatīṁ mahīm
avyayāṁ ca śrīyaṁ labdhvā
vibhavaṁ cātulaṁ bhuvi

mene 'tidurlabhaṁ puṁsāṁ
sarvaṁ tat svapna-saṁstutam
vidvān vibhava-nirvāṇaṁ
tamo viśati yat pumān
(Śrīmad Bhāgavatam 9.4.15-16)

Ambarīṣa Mahārāja was the sole proprietor of the whole world, consisting of seven islands (*sapta-dvīpavatīṁ*), meaning seven continents. This story in *Śrīmad Bhāgavatam* is scriptural evidence that at one time there was one blessed and most fortunate Vaiṣṇava emperor, Ambarīṣa Mahārāja, who became the autocrat of the whole world. If we meet someone who is wealthy, we say that he is fortunate. We say that Henry Ford was fortunate because he was one of the richest men in the world. So, in that sense, we say that Ambarīṣa Mahārāja was fortunate, because he was the sole proprietor of the whole world. He was the richest person in the whole world. For one who is the owner of the whole world, his wealth would be undecaying and of unparalleled opulence. There could not be any person equal to him. But, nonetheless, despite possessing this inexhaustible supply of wealth, all this opulence, Ambarīṣa Mahārāja had the knowledge that this opulence would not last long. It is like seeing a dream. In a dream, you may see that you have become the Prime Minister of England or the President of the United States. But when you wake up, you find yourself in your own bedroom, just lying in bed. It is all false. Like that, Ambarīṣa Mahārāja had the knowledge that whatever he had was all non-eternal. It would not last. An ordinary human being cannot even imagine becoming the sole owner of the whole world. If he were to become Henry Ford, or Tata or Birla in India, that would be sufficient. He would not want more. He cannot even think beyond that. But, in spite of Ambarīṣa getting this huge property, he understood that it had no actual substance—it was all a dream. He had the knowledge that although he presently had wealth, he could be separated from it at any time during his life. There are many very rich people, even in India. We have seen one particular person who was very wealthy. But after some years, he became a pauper, a street beggar. In this lifetime, he lost everything. Ambarīṣa Mahārāja understood that, "Although I have this wealth, I may become separated from it. Or I may leave this world and all this will remain here. Nothing will go with me. As long as I am here, I might have it. But when I die, I will not be able to take even a farthing of it." He had the knowledge that separation from this world is inevitable. He knew that anyone who thinks, "I am the owner, I am the enjoyer," will meet an infernal end.

The Supreme Lord is the only Master and Owner. We are not masters or owners. Being enveloped by the illusory energy, we think that we are masters and enjoyers. For this reason, we are being punished. We have come to this prison-house, to this world, passing through cycles of births and deaths, with the three-fold afflictions of material life. We have received this punishment because we are not the owner, but we pose as the owner. You have gone through the lectures of Most Revered Param Pūjyapāda A. C. Bhaktivedanta Svāmī Mahārāja. He said that there is a simple formula for getting peace: the Supreme Lord is the only Proprietor and Master. We claim to be masters. For instance, this Maṭha started only a few years ago. Before that time, this property belonged to somebody else who was thinking, "This is mine." Now you are saying, "It is ours." And after some time, one hundred years, one thousand years, someone will also claim it as their own. So, who is the proprietor? Who is the master? The Master is the Supreme Lord. We falsely claim to be masters. Will we accept the Supreme Lord as the only Owner and Master? We are not even the owners of our own bodies. This body also belongs to the Supreme Lord. The *śuṣma* (subtle body) also belongs to the Supreme Lord as it has come from the external potency of the Supreme Lord. *Ātmā* has come from the *parā* potency of the Supreme Lord. The potency of Kṛṣṇa and the products of that potency all belong to Kṛṣṇa—the gross body, the subtle body and the real self. Everything belongs to Kṛṣṇa. I have no right to use it for myself. It should be dedicated to the service of Kṛṣṇa. I am guilty of unrighteousness by using that which does not belong to me. Kṛṣṇa is the only Master and Enjoyer. You are not the owner of your house. You are not the owner of your wife and children. You must believe this on a practical level, not theoretical. If you actually believe it, you will immediately find peace. When you demand, "This is my house, these are my people," then you will fight with others. But if you say, "Kṛṣṇa, everything belongs to You, I have nothing," then where is the quarrel? This is the simple formula for obtaining peace.

"*Tamo viśati yat pumān:*" If you have this sort of evil thinking, that the objects of the world are for my enjoyment, then you will fall into hell. An ascetic such as myself does not earn money. Let us imagine that I collect some money from the devotees, build a Maṭha with it and then demand that, "This is mine!" People will say, "What is this? This is very strange! By our money you have built a temple and you are demanding that you are the proprietor? What is this? You should be ashamed!" But actually, we do have this sort of mentality and we fall into hell.

But Ambarīṣa Mahārāja had the knowledge that everything belongs to the Supreme Lord and nothing belongs to us. He had no attachment to anything. Why? We would not even be able to give up our attachment to a cottage, or a small shop, or even £10,000. This is because we have no taste of the sweetness of the Supreme Lord. Śukadeva Gosvāmī told Parīkṣit Mahārāja that Ambarīṣa Mahārāja had no attachment because he had tasted the sweetness of Vāsudeva:

vāsudeve bhagavati
tad-bhakteṣu ca sādhuṣu
prāpto bhāvaṁ paraṁ viśvaṁ
yenedaṁ loṣṭravat smṛtam
(*Śrīmad Bhāgavatam* 9.4.17)

Ambarīṣa Mahārāja had superior *ānanda* (bliss).

Go through the explanation given by Śrīla Bhaktivinode Ṭhākura on the following *Bhagavad-gītā* verse:

viṣayā vinivartante
nirāhārasya dehinaḥ
rasa-varjaṁ raso 'py asya
paraṁ dṛṣṭvā nivartate
(*Bhagavad-gītā* 2.59)

He says that observing a complete fast does not mean that we have given up our inclination to take food. For instance, when we first entered our Maṭha, we were advised by the Mahārājas there that if we wanted to take food on Ekādaśī, we should take very little, maybe a few pieces of fruit and some potato. But if we only took this, our stomach was always burning. So we had given things up, but what was the use of having given them up? So, now we take fruits, potato, but also curries, etc., so we do not feel that burning sensation. On Ekādaśī the *brahmacārīs* are very hungry, so they prepare what they will eat the next morning. Also, in our Maṭhas, there are "*maṭha rakṣasas*" who look after the functions of the Maṭha. If you ask them, they will tell you that no one takes rice or wheat, etc. on Ekādaśī, but on the days before and after Ekādaśī, the *brahmacārīs* are eating double! So, the inclination for taking food is not stopped by observing a fast. For that reason, *viṣayā vinivartante nirāhārasya dehinaḥ:* withdrawing the senses from the objects of the senses, in the manner of a *jñānī* or a *yogī*, is not safe.

Saubharī Ṛṣi was a great saint in the *jñānī* school of thought. He performed penance for 10,000 years under the water. We cannot remain under water for even five minutes. But, on seeing the sexual activity of the fishes there, he developed a desire to marry. He came out of the water and married fifty daughters of Māndhātā. Being a *jñānī*, he fell down from his severe penance and instead became the head of a great family. Viśvāmitra was a great *yogī*. When he came in contact with Menakā, the *apsarā* (heavenly prostitute), he also had a spiritual fall. This was because they had no taste of the sweetness of the Supreme Lord. They are performing penance, but they will fall. We all have material senses. We are attempting to enjoy the objects of those material senses and we have become entangled. If you merely stop that activity, it will not be sufficient. The cause of the material sense organs is the spiritual sense organs, and the object of the spiritual senses is Madana-Mohana—Govinda. You have an attraction for the worldly *śabda*, *sparśa*, *rūpa*—sound, touch, form, etc. But there is also transcendental, sweet sound, transcendental touch—everything—and we can taste it by means of transcendental, spiritual senses. If your existence and ego are in this material world, then your perception will be material. But if, by the Lord's grace, you can enter into the transcendental realm, then, by means of transcendental sense organs, you will experience sweet love, transcendental touch, etc.

Ambarīṣa Mahārāja had gotten a taste of the sweetness of Vāsudeva and the sweetness of His devotees and, as a result, he had no attachment to worldly things. If you have no taste of the superior *rasa*, you cannot give up material attachments. For instance, there is one kind of treacle, which is mixed with some kind of inferior quality molasses. It is not good. It is very nasty. But a person who does not have good molasses or sugar might use it, and might find that some sort of sweetness is there. He has been taught that you should not take this because it will make you ill. After many warnings, he says, "All right, I shall not take it." But, he continues to take it secretly, because he has no taste for anything better. When he is given good molasses, then he will no longer wish to take the inferior kind. Like that, when we have the taste of the sweetness of the Supreme Lord, we will become totally detached from this world. Ambarīṣa Mahārāja was indifferent to worldly things because he was getting the taste of the sweetness of Vāsudeva and His personal associates. He thought that this worldly property was like a lump of dirt, having no value. He thought like that, but we are unable to think this way because we have no superior taste. We may speak, but we have no feeling.

Being a king, how had Ambarīṣa Mahārāja acquired such love for Kṛṣṇa and His devotees? Many householders who come to our Maṭha say, "Svāmījī, we come to the Maṭha to participate in the holy functions and to hear the *sādhus*. But we have so many worries, great difficulties and so many duties to perform. For that reason, we have no time to come often."

Then I ask, "Do you have time to eat food?"

"Yes," they reply, "we have to eat or we will become weak."

"So you take breakfast?"

"Yes, I have time to take breakfast. Sometimes I take my meals to work. If I feel weak, then I cannot do my work. It is necessary."

Your *ātmā* is now sleeping. *Ātmā's* food is *ātmā*. Because *ātmā* is asleep, you feel no hunger for *ātmā—ātmā's* food. You are only conscious of the body. You think that you can afford to give time to tend to the necessities of the body. You might be very engaged in something else, but you will always take off some time to take food. How many times a day do you eat? First breakfast, then lunch, then dinner and after that maybe supper—sometimes four times a day! Like that, you are taking so much time. Necessity is the mother of invention. When you think that this is your necessity, then you give time. Your *ātmā* is now in a dormant state. It is sleeping. You have no hunger. *Ātmā* requires *ātmā* for its sustenance and maintenance. Without the touch of *ātmā*, *ātmā* cannot have satisfaction. But, "We are very busy! We are very busy! We are very busy! We are very busy! We've got no time!"

Our Guru Mahārāja used to give the instance of General Goering, the right hand man of the dictator, Adolf Hitler, who created chaos throughout the whole world—a tyrant. Once General Goering gave a statement about how he recruited candidates for the Nazi forces.

"When candidates come to apply to be admitted into the force," he said, "I divide them into four categories: clever and industrious, clever and lazy, stupid and industrious and stupid and lazy. Generally, for my force, I choose the clever and industrious, but I make the chief of the department clever and lazy."

Then he was asked, "Why? The commander then has one quality less than the others. Why have you given the highest position of Commander-in-Chief to one who is clever and lazy?"

Goering replied, "It is not in our best interest to be always engaged in war. If we give the position of commander to those who are both clever and industrious, they are incapable of remaining idle. They will always want to do something and will start fighting. For this reason, the commander must be clever and know the interests of the country, but only in extreme circumstances will he fight, not so easily. So I choose someone who is clever and lazy for the position of commander."

He continued, "Those who are stupid and lazy, I accept in small numbers. These types will do little harm. I can manage them. But if they are stupid and industrious, they will do just the opposite of what they should and I always have to make good of it after the fact. Because of this, I have to expend so much energy. So, I am one thousand per cent against the stupid and industrious.

So, to which group do we belong? Stupid and industrious: "We are very busy, very busy! We've got no time to go and associate with the *sādhus*." When you've got hunger, you shall go automatically. But, now you have no hunger.

Ambarīṣa Mahārāja had engaged all his sense organs and everything he owned for the service of Kṛṣṇa:

sa vai manaḥ kṛṣṇa-padārvindayor
vacāṁsi vaikuṇṭha-guṇānuvarṇane
karau harer mandira-mārjanādiṣu
śrutiṁ cakārācyuta-sat-kathodaye

mukunda-liṅgālaya-darśane dṛśau
tad-bhṛtya gātra-sparśe 'ṅga-saṅgamam
ghrāṇaṁ ca tad-pāda-saroja-saurabhe
śrīmat-tulasyā rasanāṁ tad-arpite

pādau hareḥ kṣetra-padānusarpane
śiro hṛṣīkeśa-padābhivandane
kāmaṁ ca dāsye na tu kāma-kāmyayā
yathottamaśloka-janāśrayā ratiḥ
(Śrīmad Bhāgavatam 9.4.18-20)

Śukadeva Gosvāmī was speaking to Mahārāja Parīkṣit: "*sa vai manaḥ kṛṣṇa-padārvindayor.*" Ambarīṣa Mahārāja engaged his mind in thinking about the Lotus Feet of Supreme Lord Śrī Kṛṣṇa. The mind is the king of all the sense organs. If the mind is concentrated on the Object of Worship, then the other senses, being subservient to it, cannot do anything except service to the Supreme Lord. So first of all, he engaged his mind in thinking about the Lotus Feet of the Supreme Lord.

"*Vacāṁsi vaikuṇṭha-guṇānuvarṇane*:" he engaged his words, his tongue, in singing the glories of Viṣṇu and the Vaiṣṇavas. "*Vaikuṇṭha*" means Viṣṇu. Viṣṇu is transcendental: *pūrṇa*. "*Viṣnu ya idam viśvam vyāpnoti iti viṣnu.*" He is Complete Reality and the Vaiṣṇavas are His pure devotees, His personal associates. You will find in the scriptures that there can be no devotion if one vilifies the *sādhus* or other persons. You have to sing their glories. This is the positive side of devotional activity. If you go on speaking ill of others, your mind will become polluted. Your mind will only find the bad qualities of those persons. So what benefit will you gain? You should govern yourself, discipline yourself, restrain yourself. You should rectify yourself. You have many defects within you. When you observe the qualities of others, you see that human beings have both defects and merits mixed together. But the *sādhu* only sees the good qualities and he ignores the bad qualities. We enslaved *jīvās* discard the good qualities and see the bad qualities. So we are not *sādhus*. *Sādhu* is *paramahaṁsa*. "*Haṁsa*" means "swan". What is the special quality of the swan? If milk is mixed with water, that swan can extract the milk from the water. He has that capacity. So, the Vaiṣṇava is *paramahaṁsa*: they take the essence of things, the good things, and they give up the bad things. So, you must sing the glories of Supreme Lord Śrī Kṛṣṇa and you must sing the glories of the devotees. Why are you taking the risk of speaking ill of anybody? It is very risky. By speaking ill of others, ultimately you are speaking ill of the Vaiṣṇavas, you are speaking ill of the Gurus, and you will be completely separated from the spiritual realm and devotional development.

"*Karau harer mandira-mārjanādiṣu*": he engaged his two hands in scrubbing the temple with water, etc. Some would say, "He is a king and he has not engaged any servant or priest to perform worship? Instead he himself is doing this. Is he a miser?" No, he is not a miser. He is serving all the Vaiṣṇavas. He knows, "This is my necessity, to serve Kṛṣṇa. If I serve Kṛṣṇa, I shall develop love for Kṛṣṇa." Wherever I shall engage my sense organs and object of the senses, I shall go to that. If I engage my sense organs in the temporary things of the world, I shall develop an attachment for those things. I shall be in bondage. Knowing this fully, Ambarīṣa was the sole owner of the whole world and he engaged everything he had for the service of Kṛṣṇa—everything. If we are not worshipping in this way, how can we claim to have love for Kṛṣṇa? He had engaged everything.

"*Śrutiṁ cakārācyuta-sat-kathodaye*:" Ambarīṣa engaged his ears in hearing the glories of the Supreme Lord. What is the meaning of "*sat-kathā*?" We will frequently engage the ears to hear professional platform speakers. There are many platform speakers like myself. From the platform he is speaking nice high, lofty words, but his life is no practical application of it. It is all idle chatter—always speaking, speaking without any practical application. We cannot teach others belief in God and worship of God if we do not worship God ourselves. Example is better than precept. There should be personal example. You should practice. You will find that if one actually practices, but does not speak anything at all, that will have actual influence upon others.

Ambarīṣa Mahārāja hears only the words of the bonafide *sādhus*. His life is dedicated to the service of hearing *sat-kathā*: actual *hari-kathā*:

yāha, bhāgavata paḍa vaiṣṇavera sthāne
(Caitanya Caritāmṛta, Antya-līlā, 5,131)

You have to hear *Bhāgavata* from a true Vaiṣṇava. Then you can get devotion.

Time is passing. So much time is passing. At any moment, we may leave this place. What will go with us? We are acquiring money, perhaps millions of dollars, and then we die. What will go with us? Everything will remain here. Nothing will go with us except devotion to Śrī Kṛṣṇa. That is our only wealth. How many of us are thinking about this?

Our Chidghanānanda *brahmacārī* once told me when I was in Chandigarh that one famous speaker on *Śrīmad Bhāgavatam* had come to Chandigarh and had been delivering lectures on Kṛṣṇa. One lady devotee had asked Chidghanānanda, "You are not going? You are a devotee. Many thousands of people have gathered there to hear this person. You should go there. You will be benefited."

Chidghanānanda replied, "I have many duties that I have been assigned by the Gosvāmīs and other senior Vaiṣṇavas. If I find time, I shall go."

Then the next day, the lady returned and approached him again. "Did you go yesterday?" she asked.

"No, no," he replied. "I've had no time. What can be done? I am at the service of my superior Vaiṣṇavas."

The third day, she asked again, "Have you gone to see the speaker?"

"No," Chidghanānanda again replied. Then he asked her, "Why are you saying that he is a great saint and that I should go to hear him? What special quality does he have that makes you say this?"

She replied, "To hear his sermon, you have to pay 10,000 rupees!"

"Oh," Chidghanānanda replied, "Then, I shall not go there! If you pay 10,000 rupees, then his sayings are very valuable. But they are valuable only in reference to 10,000 rupees. I have no time for that."

The Gauḍīya Maṭha standard is different. They are not like ordinary people. They can understand this point.

"*Mukunda-liṅgālaya-darśane dṛśau*": Ambarīṣa Mahārāja engaged his eyes to see *mukunda-liṅgālaya*, the temple where Mukunda (Kṛṣṇa) is worshipped, and also to have the vision, the *darśana*, of Mukunda. The temple includes the Deities inside the temple. Pure devotees are also temples, because Bhagavān resides within the heart of the pure devotees. So, he engaged his eyes to see the temple, the Deities and the devotees, who are also temples. As time is short and I have to leave this place tomorrow, I have no time to speak about Deities. If I were to stay here for several more days, we could discuss this fully. But you should know that you are not idolaters. You are worshippers of the Deity. It is quite different—*vigraha*:

nāma vigraha svarūpa—tina eka-rūpa
tine 'bheda' nahi—tine 'cid-ānanda-rūpa'
(Caitanya Caritāmṛta, Madhya-līlā, 17.131)

Deities are All-Existence, All-Knowledge and All-Bliss. We should believe this.

"*Tad-bhṛtya gātra-sparśe 'ṅga-saṅgamam*": Ambarīṣa Mahārāja used his sense of touch to have the touch of the lotus feet of the Vaiṣṇavas, so he could acquire devotion. "*Ghrāṇaṁ ca tad-pāda-saroja-saurabhe*": He engaged his nose in smelling the scent of Tulasī and the flowers that had been offered to the Lotus Feet of Kṛṣṇa. By these methods, he received only divine sense impressions, even through the sense of smell. He had engaged everything for the service of Kṛṣṇa. "*Śrīmat-tulasyā rasanāṁ tad-arpite*": Did he take whatever foodstuffs he found to be good? No. Whatever cannot be offered to the Supreme Lord, he would not take. Fish, flesh, eggs, onions, garlic, red lentils, etc. are prohibited in the scriptures. They cannot be offered to Viṣṇu. Ambarīṣa Mahārāja would offer only those foods that can be offered to Viṣṇu and, then, take the remnants—*prasādam*. "He is a very good person. He eats whatever is given to him." No, this is not correct thinking:

āhāra-śuddhau citta-śuddhiḥ
citta-śuddhau dhruvā smṛtir
smṛti-lambhe sarvagranthīnāṁ vipramokṣaḥ
(Chāndogya Upaniṣad 7.26.2)

If your heart is not pure, then your mind will be impure. You will not be able to meditate. *Āhāra-śuddhi*. If you eat foods that are in *tamo-guṇa*, then *tamo-guṇa* will increase. If you eat foods in *rajo-guṇa*, then *rajo-guṇa* will increase and foods in *sattva-guṇa* will increase *sattva-guṇa*. But if you take *prasādam*, it is *nirguṇa* (devoid of material qualities) and devotion will increase. We take *prasādam*. We do not even take *sattva-guṇa* foodstuffs. We are not "vegetarians." We take only *prasādam*, that which can be offered to Śrī Kṛṣṇa. Anything else, we will not take.

"*Pādau hareḥ kṣetra-padānusarpane*": He engaged his two legs in going to the holy places of pilgrimage, which are in the transcendental realm of the Supreme Lord. Then he would engage his two legs in the service of circumambulating the temple and going to fetch the various articles of worship.

"*Śiro hṛṣīkeśa-padābhivandane*": All the sense organs are in the head of the body. By praying to the Supreme Lord with your head, one engages all the sense organs at once. *Hṛṣīkeśa* is the Lord of all the senses. You have to worship Him by bowing down your head to His Lotus Feet.

"*Kāmaṁ ca dāsye na tu kāma-kāmyayā*": he had even engaged desire itself for the service of Śrī Kṛṣṇa. If there is desire to serve Kṛṣṇa and to serve the devotees, they will rescue us. If there is a desire to enjoy this world, then that desire will take us to worldly things and we will become entangled. We will go to hell. For that reason, he had engaged all that he had for the service of Kṛṣṇa, and he was filled with *kṛṣṇa-prema*. All other activities had been stopped, so that *māyā* would not be able to enter. All his sense organs were engaged for the service of Kṛṣṇa. If you are to get Kṛṣṇa, you have to do this.

Now, this is the main subject. One day, Durvāsā Ṛṣi set his holy footprints at the house of Ambarīṣa Mahārāja in Madhuvana (a part of Vṛndāvana). At that time Ambarīṣa Mahārāja observed Ekādaśī in the following way: on Daśamī (the tenth day of the lunar month), he would take only one meal, on Ekādaśī (the eleventh day of the lunar month), he would abstain from all food and on Dvādaśī (the twelfth day of the lunar month), he would take only one meal. In those days, people had the capacity to abstain from food completely on Ekādaśī. There is a fixed time to take *pāraṇa* (breaking of the Ekādaśī fast). At that time, you must take something that you have abstained from on Ekādaśī. In this way, your vow will be observed correctly. Then this is *hari-vrata*, because you are doing it for the satisfaction of Hari. On Dvādaśī, Ambarīṣa Mahārāja served all the *brāhmaṇas*, all the *sādhus* and all his others guests with gifts and *prasādam*. After serving them, he went to take *pāraṇa*.

At that moment, Durvāsā Ṛṣi unexpectedly arrived and said, "Ambarīṣa Mahārāja, I am Durvāsā."

Ambarīṣa Mahārāja replied, "I am most fortunate that such a great *brāhmaṇa sannyāsī* has come to my house. Today is Dvādaśī. I pray that you will take food here."

"Yes," Durvāsā Ṛṣi replied, "I shall take food. But first, I will go to the Yamunā to bathe. After I take my bath, I shall come here to eat."

Durvāsā Ṛṣi went to bathe. Upon seeing the pure water of the Yamunā, he became completely and ecstatically absorbed in thoughts of Brahman. He completely forgot to come back to Ambarīṣa Mahārāja's house to eat. Ambarīṣa Mahārāja began to think, "There is not much time left for *pāraṇa*. If I do not break my fast, I shall commit an offense to Hari. But if I eat before Durvāsā, I shall commit an offense to the lotus feet of the *brāhmaṇa sannyāsī* whom I have invited here to take food. This is a great dilemma." So, he sought advice from the *brāhmaṇas* who were present there. "What shall I do?" he asked. "You can take water," they advised. "By taking water, you will not be violating the honor of a guest, and you will also complete your fast and perform *pāraṇa*." So, at the advice of the *brāhmaṇas*, he took a drop of water.

But Durvāsā Ṛṣi could understand by his mystic power that Ambarīṣa Mahārāja had taken water. He thought, "Ambarīṣa Mahārāja is the emperor of the whole world. So, he has some vanity. I did not go to his house with the intention of taking food—he invited me. I am a *brāhmaṇa*, a *sannyāsī*. If one who is a *brāhmaṇa* and a *sannyāsī* is invited by a householder to eat and that householder takes food earlier than he, then the whole of society will be destroyed! Ambarīṣa Mahārāja is the emperor and also a religious-minded person and he has done this. His guests will quote this instance and others will follow his example. No, I cannot allow this. I shall give an exemplary punishment so that no man of this world will again commit this heinous offense. It is a very great sin."

Then Durvāsā Ṛṣi became enraged and said to Ambarīṣa Mahārāja, "So, you have become proud that you are the emperor of the world? I have come to you to take food. You personally invited me. You know that I am a *brāhmaṇa* and a *sannyāsī*. Even if an ordinary guest comes to you, you must give food to him. So, without your guest having been fed, you have taken food yourself? This is wrong behavior. I shall punish you!"

Durvāsā Ṛṣi plucked a hair from his head and threw it down. A goddess appeared from it, wielding a weapon to kill Ambarīṣa Mahārāja. She ran toward the king, but he did not flee. He said, "I am a householder, I am a *kṣatriya*. In all respects, I am inferior to you and you have the right to punish me. Whatever you choose to do, I accept."

But, by the standing order of Nārāyaṇa, the Sudarśana-cakra appeared. Ambarīṣa Mahārāja was the king. He was the emperor and the sole proprietor of the whole world, but he had no attachment to it. Outside people cannot understand this. So, Nārāyaṇa said, "Oh, Sudarśana-cakra, whenever Ambarīṣa is in difficulty, immediately go out and rescue him!" Sudarśana-cakra came and burnt the goddess to ashes. Then it began to chase Durvāsā Ṛṣi. Durvāsā began to flee from the burning sensation of the *cakra*. Durvāsā Ṛṣi was fleeing from one direction to another. No matter which direction he fled to, the Sudarśana-cakra followed. Durvāsā even entered the ocean, but the *cakra* came there also and immediately gave him burning pain. He felt as if he were dying from the miseries of this burning sensation of the Sudarśana-cakra. He sought refuge in a cave of Sumeru Mountain, but the *cakra* followed him into there as well.

Eventually, he went to Satya-loka to take shelter of Lord Brahmā. But Brahmā said, "This Sudarśana-cakra is unbearable. It is the punishment of Nārāyaṇa. We think we are the creators, but we are not. Only as per the direction of Nārāyaṇa have we been given the capacity to create this universe. We are under Him. We are not His superiors. We cannot stop Sudarśana-cakra. Sudarśana-cakra is as unbearable to us as it is to you."

Durvāsā Ṛṣi then went to take shelter of Mahādeva (Śiva). Durvāsā had been born from the power of Mahādeva, so actually he was the expansion of Rudra (Śiva). Rudra said to him, "You see, you think that I am the destroyer. But everything is controlled by Nārāyaṇa. By His direction, Brahmā is creating and by His direction I am destroying. I have no independent power. This Sudarśana-cakra is the punishment of Nārāyaṇa. It is not possible for me to oppose it. It is unbearable for me also. But you have come to me, so I am blessing you. Go to Nārāyaṇa in Vaikuṇṭha. He can rescue you."

Durvāsā had no desire to go to Nārāyaṇa, but he was forced to go to ask Him to save him from this intolerable burning sensation. He went to Vaikuṇṭha and fell flat on the ground, praying, "I have committed an offense, but please be kind to me. This Sudarśana-cakra is giving me so much pain! You are Acyuta! What is the meaning of Acyuta? Nobody can be detached from You! O Acyuta! If I am detached from You, then there is no significance to Your Name 'Acyuta'. Since Your Name is 'Acyuta,' You cannot be Acyuta without me. You are Acyuta, so please be kind to me."

Nārāyaṇa did not say anything.

Durvāsā Ṛṣi continued, "You are Ananta (unending)! Your every quality is Ananta! I am in so much pain, so much suffering. I have committed an offense. I admit this. But You are Ananta and Your compassion is also Ananta. If You cannot grace me, it will bring ill repute to Your Name, Ananta. So, please rescue me from this burning sensation."

Nārāyaṇa still did not utter a word.

"You are Viśvanātha! You are Jagannātha!" Durvāsā Ṛṣi prayed. "Why is Your Name Jagannātha? You are the Master of all the living beings of the world. I admit that I have committed an offense. But You are Jagannātha and I am an insignificant living being of this world. You are my Nātha (Lord) and I have come to You so that You may rescue me."

"Will You not be kind to me? The *sādhus* who worship You are always compassionate to the *jīvās* of this world. They always try to remove the afflictions of the suffering *jīvās*. They have achieved this quality by worshipping You. You have the quality of supreme compassion for the fallen souls. You are the acme of compassion. Simply by worshipping You, the *sādhus* become gracious, so will You not be gracious to me?"

Then Nārāyaṇa asked, "You have already gone to Brahmā and Mahādeva. Have they not offered you protection?"

"No," Durvāsā Ṛṣi replied, "They said they are unable to protect me. They said they could not do anything, as they are subjugated by

You. They are dependent upon You."

Nārāyaṇa then replied, "I am also dependent. I am also a servant."

"You are a servant?" Durvāsā asked in disbelief. "How can this be?"

Then Nārāyaṇa said:

ahaṁ bhakta-parādhīno
hy asvatantra iva dvija
sādhubhir grasta-hṛdayo
bhaktair bhakta-jana-priyaḥ
(Śrīmad Bhāgavatam, 9.4.63)

"I have made a promise. Whoever serves Me, in return I shall serve him in the same way. When the pure devotees serve Me, I want to give them something. I say, 'Take this,' but they never want anything from Me. I tell them, 'Take ownership of this *brahmāṇḍa*—ownership of this world, of the heavens and the netherworld.' I offer them the eighteen kinds of attainment, including emancipation. But they do not want anything except to perform service to Me. So, I have become dependent and subjugated, as I am subdued by the devotion of My devotees. I cannot do anything. '*Sādhubhir grasta-hṛdayo bhaktair bhakta-jana-priyaḥ*.' With one's heart, one can be compassionate. But My heart has been swallowed and devoured by My devotees. '*Grasta*': they have taken it. Thus, My heart is not here. It has gone to My devotees. Therefore, if you are to receive My grace, you have to go to Ambarīṣa Mahārāja. You thought Ambarīṣa Mahārāja to be a householder, a *kṣatriya*—an ordinary person:

nāham ātmānam āśāse
mad-bhaktaiḥ sādhubhir vinā
śriyaṁ cātyantikīṁ brahman
yeṣāṁ gatir ahaṁ parā
(Śrīmad Bhāgavatam, 9.4.64)

Without the *sādhus* who have love for Me, I do not want even My own Self. Nor do I want Lakṣmī Devī and all this wealth. I want only those who take absolute shelter of Me and nothing else. You think, then, that Ambarīṣa is a householder? You think that he is engrossed in worldly things and that he has vanity? You see,

ye dārāgāra-putrāpta-
prāṇān vittam imaṁ param
hitvā māṁ śaraṇaṁ yātāḥ
kathaṁ tāṁs tyaktum utsahe
(Śrīmad Bhāgavatam 9.4.65)

Ambarīṣa Mahārāja has given up his wife. He has given up his house. He has given up his sons and other relatives and his very life. He has given up the whole world for Me! How can I relinquish him? How can I? Is it possible? You are seeing him as a king. But he has given up everything for Me! Is it possible that I can forsake him? It is not possible!

mayi nirbaddha-hṛdayāḥ
sādhavaḥ sama-darśanāḥ
vaśe kurvanti māṁ bhaktyā
sat-striyaḥ sat-patiṁ yathā
(Śrīmad Bhāgavatam, 9.4.66)

A chaste wife subdues a chaste husband by her service. In the same way, a devotee has one-pointed devotion to Me. They are equal to everyone, because they see everyone in relation to their devotion to Me."

You cannot have equal vision, *sama-darśana*, when you have no devotion to the Supreme Lord. One of the *brahmacārīs* in Calcutta once told me, "When I came to Calcutta, I was rescued."

"Why? I asked."

"Because one of the female devotees there told me, 'My husband is not congenial toward this service, but I want to perform some service. So, please come once every month when my husband will not be home. I want to give something for Rādhā-Kṛṣṇa and Gaurāṅga Mahāprabhu every month, so will you please come there and take it.'"

One day the *brahmacārī* went there, but on that particular day, the husband had not gone to the office and he was there at the house. He saw that a *brahmacārī* was coming. The *brahmacārī* was afraid. When he entered, he saw the husband sitting at the table eating. At the same time, their dog was also eating—from the same dish!

The husband said, "O *brahmacārī*! By taking a saffron cloth, a man cannot acquire equal *darśana*! I am taking food with the dog! Will you also take? Simply by wearing a saffron cloth, a man cannot become a *sādhu*! See? You cannot do this? Just by ringing a bell in a temple, a man cannot become a devotee! *Sama-darśana*! There must be *sama-darśana*!"

The *brahmacārī* then became afraid that the husband might beat him. The *brahmacārī* remained silent and left the house thinking, "I have been rescued. This is not *sama-darśana*. This man is seeing a dog. He is seeing a man. This cannot be *sama-darśana*." *Sama-darśana* is not so easily obtained. Thousands of saints have performed immense penances to obtain *sama-darśana*. When we have exclusive devotion to Śrī Kṛṣṇa, then we shall see Śrī Kṛṣṇa in everything and all living beings in relation to Him. We will not see the dog, the cat or the man. We will see the Supreme Lord in every living being. That is called *sama-darśana*. "*Myā saha vartamān iti sama.*"

Nārāyaṇa told Durvāsā Ṛṣi, "You must go to Ambarīṣa Mahārāja. Only he can rescue you. I cannot rescue you because My heart is not here."

During this time, Ambarīṣa Mahārāja was feeling very dejected because Durvāsā Ṛṣi had left his home without taking any food. The king thought, "I have committed a great offense." He took only water for a full year, after which time Durvāsā Ṛṣi returned to Ambarīṣa Mahārāja. When Durvāsā Ṛṣi arrived, he paid his obeisances to Ambarīṣa Mahārāja.

The king immediately protested, "What are you doing? In all respects, you are superior to me. I am an insignificant person, a householder. Why are you bowing to me?"

"No! No!" Durvāsā Ṛṣi cried, "I have been to Brahmā, Śiva and others. I have also been to Nārāyaṇa and He sent me to you. This Sudarśana-cakra is giving me immense pain!"

Ambarīṣa Mahārāja prayed to the Sudarśana-cakra, "O Sudarśana-cakra! This *brāhmaṇa* is not at fault. It is my fault. He has the right to command me. He is innocent! Please stop giving him pain."

The *cakra* did not respond.

"I am offering you all my piety. Please stop the burning of this *brāhmaṇa*."

Still the *cakra* did not respond.

Ambarīṣa Mahārāja then pleaded, "I am not a devotee, but if I have done any service for Śrī Kṛṣṇa, please accept all of it in lieu of this punishment and release this *brāhmaṇa* from your intense heat." Then, immediately the Sudarśana-cakra stopped.

Ambarīṣa Mahārāja had given all he had to rescue the very person who had come to kill him! It is not so easy to become such a *sādhu*. It is very difficult.

Supreme Lord Śrī Kṛṣṇa was so very satisfied with Ambarīṣa Mahārāja's observance of Ekādaśī-vrata in Madhuvana-maṇḍala, that the curse of Durvāsā Ṛṣi could not touch him. According to the commentary of Śrīla Viśvanātha Cakravartī Ṭhākura, Durvāsā Ṛṣi delivered this curse specifically to create a pastime that would declare the glorious activities of Ambarīṣa Mahārāja.

SANCTIFYING THE HEART

Our Most Revered Gurudeva, Nityalīlā Praviṣṭa Oṁ Viṣṇupāda Śrī Śrīmad Bhakti Dayita Mādhava Gosvāmī Mahārāja, Founder/President of Śrī Caitanya Gauḍīya Maṭha institution, established this Calcutta Maṭha, and his objects of worship, Śrī Śrī Guru-Gaurāṅga-Rādhā-Nayananātha Jīu, appeared here by dint of his devotion. He installed the Deities during the winter season. Thereafter, our Gurudeva introduced two five-day religious meetings in the Calcutta Maṭha to celebrate the occasions of the anniversary of the installation of the Deities and Śrī Kṛṣṇa Janmāṣṭamī, the advent anniversary of Śrī Kṛṣṇa. At that time, when he was living on this earth, we were under him directly, so we had no worries. Whatever he directed was directed by Supreme Lord Śrī Kṛṣṇa. Gurudeva is the absolute counterpart of the Supreme Lord, and we were not to be worried. But, after his disappearance, we could not see him physically although, indirectly, he was still directing everything. As God is eternal, His absolute counterpart is also eternal. As long as there is the sun, the light of the sun, the quality of the sun will also be there. If the sun is eternal, its light will also be eternal. Like that, the Supreme Lord is the Supreme Eternal Entity and, therefore, His absolute counterpart is also eternal. He is grace incarnate. He graces all the deserving enslaved *jīvās* of this world.

By the grace of the Supreme Lord, we can see that His grace incarnate is the bonafide guru, His personal associate. Gurudeva, the grace incarnate of Supreme Lord Śrī Kṛṣṇa Gaurāṅga Mahāprabhu, appeared and put his holy footprints in our own place. I had no knowledge of Gauḍīya Maṭha, but he attracted me. He is the expansion of Caitanya Mahāprabhu. Caitanya Mahāprabhu sent His own personal associate here. He also went to many different places and rescued many fallen souls. We have to remember Gurudeva. Without his grace, without submission to him, without sincere belief in him, we cannot have any kind of contact with Kṛṣṇa.

Throughout the infinite planets, you will find all the pastimes of Śrī Kṛṣṇa going on continuously, one after another. In this sense, His appearance pastime is eternal:

ei-mata brahmāṇḍa-madhye sabāra 'parakāśa'
sapta-dvīpe nava-khaṇḍe yāṅhāra vilāsa
sarvatra prakāśa tiara—bhakte sukha dite
jagatera adharma nāśi' dharma sthāpite
Caitanya Caritāmṛta, Madhya-līlā 20.218-219)

There are infinite *brahmāṇḍas* and infinite planets—so many that we cannot even conceive of them. Somewhere within these *brahmāṇḍas*, He is appearing continuously. So, in this sense, His appearance is eternal. But He also appears, reveals Himself, in the sanctified heart of the *śuddha bhakta*. This is also His eternal appearance. We have to prepare ourselves so that Kṛṣṇa will think us to be qualified to get Him. Then He will appear in our hearts. Today is the day before Janmāṣṭamī—"*adhivāsa*". "*Adhivāsa*" means that we have some prior duty to perform before His appearance, so that we will be ready for Him. We have to sanctify our hearts so that Kṛṣṇa can appear there. Kṛṣṇa is already there, but we are not aware of His presence.

ceto darpaṇa mārjanaṁ bhāva-maha—dāvāgni nirvāpaṇam
śreyaḥ-kairava-candrikā-vitaraṇaṁ vidyā-vadhu-jīvanam
ānandāmbudhi-vardhanaṁ prati-padaṁ pūrṇāmṛtāsvādanaṁ
sarvātma-snapanaṁ paraṁ vigayate śrī-kṛṣṇa-saṅkīrtanam
(Śikṣāṣṭaka 1)

Supreme Lord Śrī Caitanya Mahāprabhu wrote this verse thereby instructing us how to attain the association of Kṛṣṇa. How can Kṛṣṇa appear in us? What do we have to do? "*Śrī-kṛṣṇa-saṅkīrtanam*": chant the Holy Names of Śrī-Kṛṣṇa. Then you will get everything. "You do not need to do anything to purify your mind, except to go on chanting 'Rādhā-Kṛṣṇa', Hare Kṛṣṇa *mahāmantra*. Everything will come to you." We say this repeatedly with our words but, in practice, we have no belief.

The Supreme Lord will descend into our hearts—will be revealed in our hearts—when we actually and sincerely take absolute shelter at His Lotus Feet. He will reveal Himself to the surrendered soul. If we chant with bonafide submission, we will find that everything is there in the Holy Name—Form, Attributes, everything. The Name is *saccidānanda*. Kṛṣṇa is *saccidānanda*. This realization will descend into our hearts. We might think that we will get Him by our own capacity, but He is not subservient to us. He is Self-effulgent, Self-luminous like the sun.

Svāmī Mahārāja (Śrīla A. C. Bhaktivedanta Svāmī Mahārāja) used to say, "If one is enlightened by that knowledge by which ignorance is destroyed, then that knowledge reveals everything just as the sun illuminates everything at daybreak." When the sun rises, he shows himself and everything else in proper perspective. We think *harināma* to be material sound and that we can get Kṛṣṇa by our own capacity. No! If we submit to God and His absolute counterpart, then all will be revealed.

We cannot bribe the Supreme Lord. Everything is within Him, there is nothing outside Him. Dhruva Mahārāja received the grace of the Supreme Lord. We are uttering the Name and we are not getting this grace. Why? "He is not gracing us!" we complain. No, no. The sun is giving light to all. It is shining in the filthy place, the clean place—everywhere. Some are taking advantage of it, but the majority is not taking. Nonetheless, we complain, "The sun is not blessing us."

Dhruva had firm belief. His faith was without a trace of doubt. "My mother told me that by crying the Name of Śrī Hari, I shall get Śrī Hari." He was crying, crying, crying continuously. We are not doing this. He was continuously uttering the Holy Name, completely absorbed in Hari and, whatever he saw, whether a lion, crocodile or any other beast, he embraced. They did no harm to him as he was protected from all danger. However, we have difficulty believing this. Ultimately, he received the grace of Nārada Gosvāmī.

That was an example from *Śrīmad Bhāgavatam*, but in this Kali-yuga, when we were once in Punjab, a very astounding event took place. A devotee woman was traveling by rickshaw from her shop to a remote place, about two miles away. She was wearing many gold ornaments. She traveled for some time along the well-populated road when suddenly the rickshaw driver turned away from the main road, toward a field.

"Why are you going across this field?" the lady protested. "That is the way, over there."

"No," the rickshaw driver said, "I am taking a shortcut. We will go this way." He would not heed the woman's words.

Then, the woman became afraid, thinking, "I am wearing so many golden ornaments. The driver must be greedy for them. He will rob me and kill me." For this reason, she jumped from the rickshaw and started to run away, shouting "Hah Govinda! Hah Govinda!" This is fact. We were there at the time.

To save herself, she jumped into a well. In terror, she remained in the well throughout the night, all the time uttering, "Hah Govinda!"

At dawn, the next morning, many people from the village came for their morning walk. They heard the sound of a woman's voice uttering the Holy Name. "What is this?" they asked. They followed the voice to the well and found the woman who was crying "Hah Govinda! Hah Govinda!" An extremely poisonous snake was swimming around her, circling her. "What is this?" they wondered. Then, they saw the rickshaw. A man holding a dagger lay next to it—dead. A great cry rose from the crowd and many people gathered from different places to see what had happened. By now, it was daylight and, as people came to the woman's aid, the snake left.

All the witnesses at the scene said they had never seen that snake before and, since that time, they have never seen it again. When the rickshaw driver went to kill the woman with his dagger, the snake bit him and injected him with venom, killing him instantly. After that, the same snake protected the woman throughout the night by circling her, so that no one could come near. The woman had firm belief. She did not utter any other Name, only "Govinda! Govinda! Govinda!" Even in this Kali-yuga, you can find such an event. Therefore, you should have belief.

Janmāṣṭamī and other auspicious functions at the Maṭha are "*hari-smaraṇa-mahoṭsava*" (grand celebrations dedicated to the remembrance of Hari). You will find, in a certain hymn, that the entire purpose of performing *bhajana* is to remember Kṛṣṇa. We shall destroy all evil thoughts by remembering Kṛṣṇa. We shall get everything by remembering. But, it is said in the scripture called *Vaiṣṇava Cintāmaṇi*, that it is not easy to remember, to meditate, with this material mind. It is very difficult. All the sins, vices and evil thoughts will be destroyed by remembrance of Kṛṣṇa, but it is not so easy. But, we can remember Kṛṣṇa if we utilize our lips to utter the Name. By moving these lips, we can obtain eternal benefit, but, unfortunately, we have no aptitude for this. We cannot remember Kṛṣṇa by means of the material mind.

When we are able to remember Kṛṣṇa by loudly and continuously performing *harināma*, and that remembrance is revealed in our hearts, then we will be entitled to perform *bhajana* in a secluded place. Not now. Śrī Caitanya Mahāprabhu is teaching us. Our Bhaktisiddhānta Sarasvatī Ṭhākura is teaching us. If our Gurudeva ever saw some devotees dancing and chanting the Holy Name, he would show them great respect. "They are expressing their hearts! Hari bol!" In order to gain some respect, name and fame, I was also dancing. "Ah! Very good!" Gurudeva would say. He would be pleased with me although I was doing it to receive praise. Inside, I had no feeling, no want for Kṛṣṇa, and no perturbation of heart. I did it only to get respect from others. Nonetheless, Gurudeva was so satisfied. Why? This you have to understand. "*Kīrtana prabhāve smarana haībe*" (Śrīla Bhakti Siddhānta Sarasvatī Ṭhākura). Remembrance of Bhagavān comes from constant chanting of the Holy Name.

Prahalāda told all the demon boys, "Why are you afraid? There is no difficulty in worshipping Kṛṣṇa. You should just utter the Name. You are calling your father and your mother without difficulty. Call Him and He will be satisfied. There is no difficulty. He is within you. He has affection for you. You will find the affection of crores of mothers in Śrī Hari." Here in this world, one always encounters difficulty when trying to please another person, but Kṛṣṇa is not at all difficult to please. With a sincere heart, utter His Name.

In your household life, you wile away the time for nothing, for worldly things. If you are also gossiping about these things here in the temple, then why have you come? The temple is for the worship of Kṛṣṇa, nothing else. You should think about this. Why have you come here? Have you spent so much money to come here only to gossip about worldly things?

What is *bhagavān-bhajana*?

śravaṇaṁ kīrtanaṁ dhyānaṁ harer adbhuta-karmaṇaḥ
janma-karma-guṇānāṁ ca tad-arthe 'khila-ceṣṭitam
(Śrīmad Bhāgavatam, 11.3.27)

Once, our Guru Mahārāja was in Vraja-maṇḍala performing *parikrama*. Generally, our Guru Mahārāja would remain in front to perform *kīrtana*, guiding the other devotees. On this particular occasion, Guru Mahārāja was held up with work at some place and would not be able to come until later. At the front of the procession, all the Vaiṣṇavas were chanting the Holy Name and the others were answering him back. But, at the back of the procession, there were so many devotees who were idly gossiping about worldly things. They did not know that Guru Mahārāja was coming up from the rear. When Guru Mahārāja came up to them, he said, "Oh! Your whole life's fortune has been destroyed! At this great procession you are also gossiping about worldly things? Then they quickly started chanting, "Rādhe Govinda! Rādhe Govinda!" What is the reason why we have spent so much money to come and be here? Is it to give our energy to worldly things? If we hear about Kṛṣṇa, we shall go to Kṛṣṇa. If we hear about worldly things, we shall go to worldly things. If we sing about Kṛṣṇa, we shall go to Kṛṣṇa. If we speak about Kṛṣṇa, we shall go to Kṛṣṇa. If we remember Kṛṣṇa, our minds will go there. If we devote all our sense organs for the service of Śrī Kṛṣṇa, we shall go to Him. This is called *bhajana*. If we go on expending all our energy for worldly things, while remaining externally in the Maṭha, what benefit will we receive?

Tomorrow, Kṛṣṇa will appear. He will appear in the shrine of our hearts. He is there within us and He will appear there. So, today, on this *adhivāsa tithi*, we have to clear the heart and mind so that Kṛṣṇa will come and sit there. Kṛṣṇa does not take His seat in an impure, dirty place. Kṛṣṇa is the Holiest. We have to prepare our hearts, purify our hearts. There should be no desire other than the service of Śrī Kṛṣṇa. If there should be any other desire, then that heart is impure. As long as impure thoughts are there, Kṛṣṇa will not appear.

In Puruṣottama-dhāma (Purī), during the time of the car festival (Ratha-yātrā), Lord Jagannātha travels from His temple in Purī to the Guṇḍicā temple, a distance of about two miles. Caitanya Mahāprabhu explains that the Guṇḍicā temple is Vṛndāvana and the Jagannātha temple is Kurukṣetra. During a solar eclipse, people go to

Kurukṣetra to bathe and perform other rituals. In the scriptures, you will find descriptions of the immense glories of this practice. During the time of Kṛṣṇa's pastimes on Earth, there was a solar eclipse where Kṛṣṇa came from Dvārakā to Kurukṣetra with all His personal associates. At that time, Kṛṣṇa was the King, Emperor and Sole Proprietor of Dvārakā. All His subjects, consorts and personal associates were very eager to go to Kurukṣetra during the solar eclipse so they could bathe, perform *sāndhya* and other rituals. If they could perform these sacrifices with the *brāhmaṇas*, they could get immense fruits. To fulfill this desire of His subjects, Kṛṣṇa said, "All right, we shall go." So, all the numerous subjects, consorts and personal associates came to Kurukṣetra. Kṛṣṇa intentionally invited everyone except the Vrajavāsis—the devotees of Vraja.

Nārada Gosvāmī was very shocked by this. He approached Kṛṣṇa, saying, "The Vrajavāsis love You so much. They are experiencing extreme separation grief by not seeing You. You are inviting everyone in the whole world but You are not inviting the Vrajavāsis? What offense are they guilty of? Have they committed an offense by loving You? I cannot tolerate this!"

Then Kṛṣṇa said, "They are our own people. No one has to send invitations to one's own. Parents do not invite their children, and vice versa. They are our own. Outside people are invited. How can I invite the Vrajavāsis? You are right, I intentionally did not invite them because they are saturated with love for Me. They have no interest in performing sacrifices to obtain mundane benefits. If they come, the results of all these ritual practices will be destroyed. For this reason, I have not invited them."

Although not invited, the Vrajavāsis came to learn that Kṛṣṇa was coming to Kurukṣetra. The Vrajavāsis thought, "Kurukṣetra is much closer to Vraja-maṇḍala than Dvārakā is. We should avail ourselves of this rare opportunity to see Kṛṣṇa! We can have *darśana* of Kṛṣṇa! We should not miss this chance!"

But, they could not venture to go there. Why? They thought, "Kṛṣṇa has become the Emperor. His standard is very high, and we are merely cowherd men and women. We are poor people. Perhaps Kṛṣṇa has forgotten us. If we go there, He will not recognize us. Someone of very high position will not come to see ordinary people like us. Previously He was a cowherd boy in our Vraja-dhāma, but now He has become King. But, we are extremely grief-stricken. We cannot tolerate this separation."

Thinking like this, the Vrajavāsis reasoned, "A man might forget everything else, but he will never forget his parents, even if they live far away. If Nanda Mahārāja and Yaśodā go there, then Kṛṣṇa will bow down to them and make obeisances." So they went to Nanda Mahārāja, saying, "Kṛṣṇa is coming to Kurukṣetra! We are too grief-stricken with separation grief. We have not seen Him for such a long time but we do not have the courage to go there. We do not know if Kṛṣṇa will give us the opportunity to see Him, as His present standard of living is so high. But if His parents go there, then Kṛṣṇa will come to them as their son and offer obeisances."

Then Nanda Mahārāja and Yaśodā said, "No, no. This is not correct. He has not come here for such a long time! He has so many consorts and servants serving Him there. He is so wealthy now. His wives are also wealthy. We are only cowherd men and women. We have nothing. After so long, how can we go? If we go there, will He come to see us? If we go to Kurukṣetra and are deprived of seeing Kṛṣṇa, we shall die!"

When Kṛṣṇa, the Emperor of Dvārakā entered Kurukṣetra, so many cavalry units, elephants, horses, etc. accompanied Him. Only those who had permission were allowed to go to speak with Him. He was surrounded by servants. There were four gatekeepers, one in each direction. The King's parents, Vasudeva and Devakī were also there. The *brāhmaṇas* had gone to start the sacrifices. So, no one was permitted to disturb the King.

Nanda Mahārāja, Yaśodā Devī and all the cowherd boys and other friends of Kṛṣṇa approached where He was. Nobody acknowledged them. Armed forces, cavalry and elephants surrounded Kṛṣṇa. Nanda Mahārāja approached one of the guards. "I have come to see my beloved son," he said.

"Who is your beloved son?" a guard asked him.

"Kṛṣṇa."

"How is that? You are a poor person. He is the King! His parents are already here—Vasudeva and Devakī. We do not believe you! From where have you come? Why are you claiming that He is your son? We do not believe you!"

Nanda Mahārāja cried, "I shall die!"

The guard said, "I am doing my work as per the order of the King. If I do anything against His orders, I shall be dismissed. Do you have a permit?"

"No."

"Then I cannot let you in," the guard replied.

Then all the cowherd boys, carrying their small cow prods, cried, "My friend! My bosom friend! Kanhaiyā!"

"What? He is the King! His friends are like this? You are paupers! I do not believe you!"

Then the *gopīs* cried, "We are the consorts of Kṛṣṇa!"

"What? The consorts are already there. Satyabhāmā, Rukmiṇī and all the other queens are there! From where have you come? Show me some permit from the King or His Prime Minister!"

Then, Yaśodā Devī said, "I told you that if I go to Kurukṣetra and I am deprived of seeing Kṛṣṇa, I shall die! I have nothing left. My life is finished!" She cried loudly, "Gopāla!" and fell unconscious.

At that time, Kṛṣṇa was with the *brāhmaṇas*, who requested Him to start the sacrifice. Kṛṣṇa removed all His royal garments and became a small, naked boy, crying, "Mother! O Mommy! Mommy! Mommy!" He cried and cried and cried and ran to sit on the lap of

Yaśodā Devī. Now, without Kṛṣṇa's presence, all the ritual sacrifices were destroyed. By hearing one single call from Yaśodā Devī, Kṛṣṇa could not remain there.

Then Kṛṣṇa met the *gopīs* and the others. The *gopīs* attracted Kṛṣṇa. They said, "We are not very happy seeing You here. There are so many cavalrymen, elephants and chariots—we should go to Vṛndāvana. There, it is sweet. All this is Your majestic aspect. So, please allow us the opportunity to see You in better circumstances by coming with us to Vṛndāvana. Please do not remain here! "*He Gopīnātha*! *He Gopīnātha*! *Vṛndāvane calo*! *He Gopīnātha*!"

In that mood of the *gopīs*, saturated with *gopī-bhāva*, Caitanya Mahāprabhu pulled the chariot from the Jagannātha temple (Kurukṣetra) toward Guṇḍicā (Vṛndāvana). During the chariot festival, Kṛṣṇa, Baladeva and Subhadra make the trip in three chariots. The day before the festival, Caitanya Mahāprabhu told the devotees, "You see, Kṛṣṇa will come to the Guṇḍicā temple tomorrow. You must come with Me and cleanse this temple." "Cleansing the temple" means that outside you must remove all the thorns and rubbish and trim the grass, etc. You must clear the path of any stones and sweep away all the dust with a broom. But, it also means that you are to engage your sense organs for the service of Kṛṣṇa. If you do not engage your sense organs, you will not get Him. For this reason, you have to clear your heart of all desire for the attainment of material benefits both here and in the hereafter in heaven. If such desire is there, Kṛṣṇa will not come. This desire for non-eternal benefits and emancipation, the desire to merge yourself in formless Brahman, the desire to merge yourself in Paramātmā, these sorts of desires will deter you from going to Kṛṣṇa. Kṛṣṇa will not come to you. For this reason, you have to clear all of this away—these desires are like hard stones. Outside, you clear them away with brooms and all the devotees bring earthen pots full of water to wash everything.

After this, there should be no desire for name and fame and other such things. All of this should be totally removed. For this reason, Caitanya Mahāprabhu, with the help of His own *uttri* (cloth that a *sannyāsī* wears around his neck), scrubbed the inside of the temple. There should not be any kind of material desires within the heart, not even those hidden secretly. Then Kṛṣṇa will come tomorrow.

Kṛṣṇa is coming here from the Jagannātha temple, and you have to clear these unwanted things away. This means that you have to clear your mind. There should be no other desire except desire for Kṛṣṇa. Kṛṣṇa is coming to Vṛndāvana. Kṛṣṇa is the only Autocrat there. No other ideas, forces or persons should dominate your heart, except Kṛṣṇa. So, you have to make your heart the same as Vṛndāvana, where Kṛṣṇa is solely dominant. He is the Sole Proprietor. Caitanya Mahāprabhu says, "I have made this mind Vṛndāvana, so that Kṛṣṇa will be free—free to perform all of His pastimes and sporting activities." You have to make your mind Vṛndāvana. No one else should be allowed to enter and no other thoughts should be allowed.

Now, you are staying in a room and outside you have placed a big sign that says, "Welcome." So, others see the sign and say, "Oh, welcome," and they come to your door. But the door is closed and behind the door there are many chairs, tables etc. In fact, the room is completely filled with furniture! They cannot even open the door. So, they go away, disappointed. Outside, your sign says, "Welcome," and you are thinking that you are welcoming Kṛṣṇa. But, when Kṛṣṇa comes, you have thoughts in your mind of wife, children, house, money, name, fame and other things. All these things have filled up your heart. Kṛṣṇa will come and then go back. You have to clear your mind, your heart, for Him. Clear away all attachment to non-eternal things. Then Kṛṣṇa will come tomorrow.

We have to perform *harināma*. This is the best method. So, in these days leading up to the advent of Śrī Kṛṣṇa, we should perform *harināma saṅkīrtana*. We should not do this to show off to others. We have to do our own *bhajana*. We must call and call Kṛṣṇa from the core of the heart. The days should be spent performing *saṅkīrtana*. Then our minds will be cleansed and Kṛṣṇa may appear. If you want Kṛṣṇa, you have to remove all things that are not Kṛṣṇa. This is "*adhivāsa*".

Caitanya Mahāprabhu has taught us that you will get everything, all kinds of attainments by means of the Holy Name. He made all the devotees chant the Holy Name, being careful to avoid the tenfold offenses. You are not to engage in meditation or any other kind of practice. Your mind will be cleansed. All the unwanted desires will be removed: "*ceto darpaṇa mārjanaṁ*." You have multifarious desires, but if you perform *saṅkīrtana*, the first attainment is that your desires will be removed. When these desires are gone, so too will be the pangs of threefold suffering—miseries. The desires are the miseries. As long as you have desires, should there be some hindrance to the fulfillment of these desires, your mind will become upset. For this reason, when the desires are removed, there will be no afflictions and Kṛṣṇa will appear. Kṛṣṇa is All-Good. After that, you will have a relationship with Kṛṣṇa, thinking, "I am of Kṛṣṇa." With love, you will utter the Holy Name and you will be drowned in the ocean of ambrosia—bliss—and, at every step, you will have the taste of that sweet transcendental ambrosia of the Supreme Lord.

About the Author

Śrīla Bhakti Ballabh Tīrtha Gosvāmī Mahārāja

His Holiness Śrīla Bhakti Ballabh Tīrtha Gosvāmī Mahārāja was born in 1924 in Assam, India, on Rāma-navami, the most auspicious appearance day of Bhagavān Lord Rāmacandra. Having been brought up in a pious environment, he developed a strong inclination to search for truth, which led him to take up the study of philosophy at Calcutta University.

After completing his MA in philosophy in 1947, he came in contact with his spiritual master, Śrīla Bhakti Dayita Mādhava Gosvāmī Mahārāja, and immediately became attracted by his divinely powerful personality. Śrīla Mādhava Mahārāja was one of the foremost followers of the illustrious preceptor of the pure devotional *bhakti* school, Śrīla Bhaktisiddhānta Sarasvatī Ṭhākura. From that time onward, Śrīla Tīrtha Mahārāja completely dedicated his life to the service of his guru. Soon he became Secretary of the devotional institution Śrī Caitanya Gauḍīya Maṭha, which has over twenty *āśramas* in India alone. He took *sannyāsa*, the vow of renunciation, in 1961.

After the disappearance of Śrīla Mādhava Gosvāmī Mahārāja in 1979, Śrīla Tīrtha Mahārāja was appointed his successor as *ācārya* of the Maṭha. During his lifetime, he received the blessings and association of many of Śrīla Bhaktisiddhānta's prominent followers, such as Śrīla Bhakti Promode Purī Gosvāmī Mahārāja, Śrīla Bhakti Hṛdaya Bon Gosvāmī Mahārāja, Śrīla Bhakti Rakṣaka Śrīdhara Gosvāmī Mahārāja, Akiñcana Kṛṣṇa dāsa Bābājī Mahārāja and many others.

For the last five decades, Śrīla Bhakti Ballabh Tīrtha Gosvāmī Mahārāja has been engaged in preaching the philosophy of Śrī Caitanya Mahāprabhu to counter the modern trend toward violence and cruelty, and to bring about unity of hearts among all, irrespective of race, creed or religion. Śrīla A.C. Bhaktivedanta Svāmī Mahārāja had requested Śrīla Tīrtha Mahārāja to accompany him to the USA just prior to his launching of the Kṛṣṇa consciousness movement in the West in 1965. As he was, at that time, engaged in the service of his Gurudeva as secretary of Śrī Caitanya Gauḍīya Maṭha, Śrīla Tīrtha Mahārāja humbly declined. Since 1997, however, at the request of Śrīla Bhakti Promode Purī Gosvāmī Mahārāja, he has been traveling the globe several months a year, enlivening all who come in contact with his humble, sweet personality, extraordinary *kīrtana* and message of divine love. To date, his preaching travels outside India have taken him around the world, including the UK, Holland, France, Spain, Italy, Austria, Germany, Slovenia, Russia, the Ukraine, Singapore, Malaysia, Indonesia, Australia, Hawaii and throughout the continental US. Everyone is attracted by his eloquent, insightful and, most of all, purely devotional discourses.

His Holiness Śrīla Tīrtha Mahārāja, during his US tour in 1997, addressed the United Nations' "World Peace Prayer Society," and "World Conference on Religion and Peace" in New York City, offering them a succinct outline for world peace based upon the spiritual tenets of the ancient Vedas. His preaching programs over the past years have also included many interesting dialogues with prominent Catholic, Protestant, Jewish, Hindu and Baha'i theologians, in such diverse settings as universities, interfaith groups, churches, Hindu temples and a wide variety of metaphysical and private educational centers. All are invariably won over by his gentle and affectionate nature, combined with his resolute faith in Guru-Vaiṣṇava-Bhagavān. He has also spoken on the sublime teachings of Śrī Caitanya Mahāprabhu on many radio and television programs, including a thought provoking interview on BBC radio in 2000, which was broadcast worldwide.

In addition to his role as *ācārya* of Śrī Caitanya Gauḍīya Maṭha, Śrīla Bhakti Ballabh Tīrtha Gosvāmī Mahārāja serves as the beloved *ācārya* of GOKUL (Global Organization of Krishnachaitanya's Universal Love), which he founded in 1997. He has also served as Vice-President of the World Vaiṣṇava Association (WVA). Working eighteen hours a day, he is incessantly engaged in the service of humanity as a teacher of Vedic wisdom and the philosophy of *bhakti-yoga*. He is also presently engaged in writing articles and books of a profound nature in his native languages as well as in English. To date, his English publications include the books *Śuddha Bhakti, Sages of Ancient India, A Taste of Transcendence* and *Śrī Gaura Pārṣada.*

GLOSSARY

Sanskrit Pronunciation Guide

Vowels

a—like the *a* in org*a*n or the *u* in b*u*t
ṛ—like *ree* in *ree*d ā—like the
a in f*a*r, but held twice as long as short *a*
ḷ—like *l* followed by *ṛ* (*lṛ*)
i—like the *i* in p*i*n e—like the *e* in th*ey*
ī—like the *i* in p*i*que, but held twice as long as short *i*
ai—like the *ai* in *ai*sle
u—like the *u* in p*u*sh o—like the *o* in g*o*
ū—like the *u* in r*u*le, but held twice as long as short *u*
au—like the *ow* in h*ow*

Consonants

k—as in *k*ite
d—as in *d*ove, but with tongue against the teeth
kh—as in Ec*kh*art
dh—as in re*d-h*ot, but with tongue against the teeth
g—as in *g*ive
n—as in *n*ut, but with tongue against the teeth
gh—as in di*g-h*ard
p—as in *p*ine ṅ—as in si*ng*
ph—as in u*ph*ill (not pronounced like *f*)
c—as in *ch*air
b—as in *b*ird
j—as in *j*oy
bh—as in ru*b-h*ard
jh—as in he*dgeh*og
m—as in *m*other
ñ—as in ca*ny*on
y—as in *y*es
ṭ—as in *t*ub, but with tongue against the roof of the mouth
r—as in *r*un
ṭh—as in ligh*t-h*eart, but with tongue against the roof of the mouth
l—as in *l*ight
ḍ—as in *d*ove, but with tongue against the roof of the mouth
v—as in *v*ine
ḍh—as in re*d-h*ot, but with tongue against the roof of the mouth
ś (palatal)—as in the *s* in the German word sprechen
ṇ—as in *n*ut, but with tongue against the roof of the mouth
ṣ (cerebral)—as the *sh* in *sh*ine
t—as in *t*ub, but with tongue against the teeth
s (dental)—as in *s*un
th—as in ligh*t-h*eart, but with tongue against the teeth
h—as in *h*ome

Special Letters

ṁ (anusvāra)—a resonant nasal like the *n* in the French word *bon*
ḥ (visarga)—a final, echoed h-sound: *aḥ* is pronounce like *aha*; *iḥ* like *ihi*

Glossary of Sanskrit Terms and Names

A

ABHIṢEKA
bathing or installation of Deities.

ĀCĀRYA
one who teaches by his own example; a spiritual master.

A. C. BHAKTIVEDANTA SVĀMĪ MAHĀRĀJA
one of the leading disciples of Śrīla Bhaktisiddhānta Sarasvatī Ṭhākura. He established the International Society for Krishna Consciousness throughout the world in the 1960's.

ACYUTA
One of the holy names of Śrī Kṛṣṇa, meaning that Person from Whom no one can be detached; the All-Unifying Spiritual Principle.

ADHIVĀSA
the day before a holy appearance day of the Supreme Lord.

ADVAITĀCĀRYA PRABHU
expansion of Mahāviṣṇu and Sadā-Śiva; it was due to his prayers that Śrī Caitanya Mahāprabhu appeared in the world. See also pañcatattva.

AGNI-HOTRA
a Vedic fire sacrifice performed daily by an agni-hotri-brāhmaṇa.

AGNI-HOTRI-BRĀHMAṆA
a brāhmaṇa who performs Vedic fire sacrifices daily.

AJĀMILA
brāhmaṇa who was saved from the messengers of the god of death by calling out the Name of Nārāyaṇa. His biography is narrated in the 6th Canto of Śrīmad Bhāgavatam.

AMBARĪṢA MAHĀRĀJA
king who dedicated all he had to the Supreme Lord and, as a result, was saved by Viṣṇu from the wrath of the brāhmaṇa, Durvāsa Muni. His biography is narrated in the 9th Canto of Śrīmad Bhāgavatam.

ĀNANDA
bliss; see also Saccidānanda.

ANANTA-ŚEṢA
manifestation of Viṣṇu Who, in the form of a huge serpent, holds all the worlds on His head as if they were no heavier than mustard seeds.

ANTARAṄGĀ-ŚAKTI
the internal potency of the Supreme Lord; see parā potency.

Aparā potency
the inferior or material potency of the Supreme Lord (māyā); the material world, comprised of the five gross elements, namely earth, water, fire, air and ether and also of the three subtle elements, namely mind, intelligence and perverted ego, is the outcome of this inferior potency. See also Bahiraṅgā-śakti.

Araṇi
a type of sacred wood used in a Vedic fire sacrifice (agni-hotra) to start the fire.

Āratika
daily, ceremonial offerings of various paraphernalia to the temple Deities, to the accompaniment of kīrtana.

Arjuna
the third of the five Pāṇḍava brothers. He was the son of Kuntī Devī. He is renowned for his prowess as a great military hero and archer. He is the intimate friend and disciple of Supreme Lord Śrī Kṛṣṇa, to whom the Supreme Lord spoke the immortal words of Bhagavād-gītā on the battlefield of Kurukṣetra.

Artha
(1) wants or requirements; (2) wealth.

Āśrama
(1) any of the four orders of life within the varṇāśrama system, (namely, brahmacārya, gṛhastha, vānaprastha and sannyāsa); (2) a religious shelter.

Ātmā
the eternal spirit soul; the real self. See also jīvātmā.

Avadhūta
a person devoid of any material desire or interest in worldly things.

B

Bahiraṅgā-śakti
external potency of the Supreme Lord comprising the world of matter (māyā).

Baladeva/Balarāma
first plenary expansion of Kṛṣṇa; the son of Rohiṇī and elder brother of Kṛṣṇa. In Caitanya-līlā, He appears as Lord Nityānanda Prabhu.

Bhaga
power or opulence. See Bhagavān.

Bhagavad-gītā
also called "Gītopāniṣad", the Bhagavad-gītā comprises the first chapter of the Bhīṣma Parva of the Mahābhārata, wherein Supreme Lord Śrī Kṛṣṇa explains the different processes of self-realization to his friend and disciple, Śrī Arjuna. The concepts of karma, jñāna and bhakti are discussed in great detail.

Bhagavān
the Supreme Lord, Who possesses six mystic opulences, or Bhagas, in full, namely: all

strength, all fame, all wealth, all beauty, all knowledge and all renunciation.

BHĀGAVATA-DHARMA
see sanātana dharma.

BHĀGAVATA PURĀṆA
see Śrīmad Bhāgavatam.

BHAJANA
(1) worship of the Supreme Lord; (2) a type of devotional song.

BHAKTA
a devotee.

BHAKTA-VĀTSALYA MŪRTI
the form of Śrī Kṛṣṇa's profound affection for His devotee.

BHAKTI
devotion to one's object of worship.

BHAKTI DAYITA MĀDHAVA MAHĀRĀJA
dīkṣā guru of Śrīla Bhakti Ballabh Tīrtha Mahārāja. He was the disciple of Śrīla Bhaktisiddhānta Sarasvatī Ṭhākura and the founder/ācārya of Śrī Caitanya Gauḍīya Maṭha.

BHAKTI PRAMODE PURĪ MAHĀRĀJA
śikṣā guru of Śrīla Bhakti Ballabh Tīrtha Mahārāja. He was the disciple of Śrīla Bhaktisiddhānta Sarasvatī Ṭhākura and the founder/ācārya of Śrī Gopīnātha Gauḍīya Maṭha.

BHAKTI-RASĀMṚTA-SINDHU
definitive devotional treatise, written by Śrīla Rūpa Gosvāmī, that methodically analyzes the principles of bhakti and the variety of loving sentiments found in spiritual relationships (rasas).

BHAKTISIDDHĀNTA SARASVATĪ ṬHĀKURA
Paramgurudeva of Śrīla Bhakti Ballabh Tīrtha Mahārāja. He was the founder of the Śrī Gauḍīya and Śrī Caitanya Maṭhas and the pioneer of the present Kṛṣṇa-Bhakti movement throughout the world.

BHAKTIVINODE ṬHĀKURA
the father of Śrīla Bhaktisiddhānta Sarasvatī Ṭhākura. In the 19th century, he revived the pure practice and scriptures of Gauḍīya Vaiṣṇavism, which were being misinterpreted by various pseudo-sects. He initiated the spread of Vaiṣṇavism to the West by sending copies of Vaiṣṇava literatures to prominent thinkers of the time, such as Ralph Waldo Emerson and Henry David Thoreau.

BHARATA MAHĀRĀJA
a great devotee of the Lord. He was the eldest son of Ṛṣabhadeva who, after renouncing his kingship of the world, became attached to a deer and subsequently took birth again as a deer. However, he attained spiritual perfection in his next life as Jaḍa Bharata. His biography is narrated in the 5th Canto of Śrīmad Bhāgavatam.

BHĪMA
the second of the five Pāṇḍava brothers, renowned for his incredible strength.

BHOGA
sensuous enjoyment.

BHṚGU MUNI
a Brahmavādi Ṛṣi, who was born directly from Brahmā; the patriarch of the Bhṛgu dynasty.

BRAHMĀ
born from the lotus-naval of Viṣṇu, he was the first created being of the universe. Directed by the Lord, he created all the life forms in the universe and is the ruler of the mode of passion (rajo-guṇa).

BRAHMACĀRĪ
a celibate student; one of the āśramas of the varṇāśrama system.

BRAHMAN
the impersonal, all-pervasive aspect of the Supreme Lord.

BRĀHMAṆA
the intellectual class; their function is to maintain the Vedic principles and to ensure the spiritual upliftment of society; one of the varṇas of the varṇāśrama system.

BRAHMĀṆḌA
any one of the uncountable material universes.

BRAHMA-SAṀHITĀ
ancient scripture consisting of beautiful and elaborate prayers offered by Lord Brahmā to Śrī Kṛṣṇa at the beginning of creation, of which the only surviving chapter is the fifth chapter. It was rediscovered in South India by Śrī Caitanya Mahāprabhu.

BRAHMA-VAIVARTA PURĀṆA
purāṇa containing, among other things, the story of Kṛṣṇa displaying his Māyā potency to Nārada Muni and also the story of Tulāsī Devī.

C

CAITANYA-LĪLĀ
the divine pastimes of Śrī Caitanya Mahāprabhu and His associates.

CAITANYA MAHĀPRABHU
Lord Kṛṣṇa's incarnation in the Kali-yuga, who appeared in Navadvīpa-dhāma, West Bengal, in the late 15th century. He inaugurated the practice of saṅkīrtana, the yuga-dharma for Kali-yuga.

CAITANYA BHĀGAVATA
one of the sacred literatures narrating the holy life and pastimes of Śrī Caitanya Mahāprabhu, written in the 16th century by Śrī Vṛndāvana dāsa Ṭhākura.

CAITANYA-CARITĀMṚTA
one of the sacred literatures narrating the holy life and pastimes of Śrī Caitanya

Mahāprabhu, written in the late 16th century by Kṛṣṇadāsa Kavirāja Gosvāmī Mahārāja.

CAITANYA-MANJUSA
a commentary on Śrīmad Bhāgavatam written by the great Vaiṣṇava saint Śrīnātha Cakravartī.

CATUR-YUGA
a cycle of four eras, or yugas, totaling 4,320,000 years. See also Satya-yuga, Tretā-yuga, Dvāpara-yuga and Kali-yuga.

CETANA
(1) a conscious entity or the principle of consciousness; (2) the Supreme Consciousness, Śrī Kṛṣṇa; (3) an individual spirit soul.

CHĀNDOGYA UPANIṢAD
so titled because of its association with the *Sāma* Veda, the Veda of chants. One of the eleven principal Upaniṣads.

CIT
knowledge or the principle of consciousness; see also Saccidānanda

CRORE
ten million.

D

DARŚANA-ŚĀSTRA
(1) eternally existing truth that can only be seen and understood by dint of self-realization, and not by means of mundane reasoning and argument; (2) self-revealed scripture (śāstra),

DAYĀ
mercy; one of the four kinds of piety: tapaḥ, śaucam, dayā, and satyam (austerity, cleanliness, mercy and truthfulness).

DEMIGOD
a personality deputed by the Supreme Lord, Śrī Kṛṣṇa, to control a specific aspect of the material creation. Indra, Brahmā and Śiva are all examples of demigods.

DEVAHŪTI
mother of Kapiladeva and wife of Kardama Muni.

DEVARĀJA
see Indra.

DHARMA
(1) the intrinsic nature of a thing; (2) the actual function or duty of an individual; (3) occupational duties within the varṇāśrama system.

DHARMA-RĀJA
see Yamarāja.

Dhṛtarāṣṭra
blind king who was the father of the Kauravas, the protagonists in the Kurukṣetra war.

Dhruva
famous boy saint who, wishing to regain his lost kingdom, performed great penance to propitiate Lord Viṣṇu. Instead, he ultimately attained devotion to Lord Viṣṇu's Lotus Feet. His holy biography is narrated in the 4th Canto of Śrīmad Bhāgavatam.

Dhyānam
engaging one's mind in meditation.

Dīkṣā
(1) transcendental spiritual knowledge; (2) the process of initiation of a sincere disciple, whereby the guru imparts spiritual knowledge capable of destroying all the disciple's sins and enabling him to realize the ultimate goal of life: kṛṣṇa-prema.

Dīkṣā guru
the spiritual master who gives dīkṣā initiation (mantra-dīkṣā) to the disciple.

Draupadī
chaste wife of the five Pāṇḍavas.

Duḥśāsana
evil-minded personality who attempted to denude Draupadī in the court of the Kurus.

Durvāsā Ṛṣi
great sage and mystic who is an expansion of Lord Śiva. He is famous for his sometimes-wrathful curses. One of these pastimes is related in the story of Mahārāja Ambarīṣa in the 9th Canto of Śrīmad Bhāgavatam.

Duryodhana
envious, eldest son of Dhṛtarāṣṭra. He is the main protagonist in the Kurukṣetra war.

Dvāpara-yuga
the third of the four eras (catur-yuga) lasting 864,000 years. The lifespan of a human being during Dvāpara-yuga was 1,000 years. The yuga-dharma of the Dvāpara-yuga was deity worship. Two of the four kinds of piety (dayā and satyam or mercy and truthfulness) were present during this era. Lord Kṛṣṇa appeared and the end of the Dvāpara-yuga.

E

Ekādaśī or Ekādaśī-tithi
the eleventh day after either the full or new moon.

Ekādaśī-vrata
the vow observed on Ekādaśī. Generally, on that day, one abstains from all grains and pulses (lentils, beans), as well as certain other items. The vow of Ekādaśī is to remain near Kṛṣṇa in all one's activities.

G

GADĀDHARA PAṆḌITA
incarnation of Śrīmatī Rādhārāṇī in Caitanya-līlā. See also Pañcatattva.

GĀṆḌĪVA
Arjuna's legendary, powerful bow, given to him by the demigod, Varuṇa.

GAURA-NITĀI
Śrī Caitanya Mahāprabhu and His most intimate companion, Lord Nityānanda Prabhu. They are expansions of Śrī Kṛṣṇa and Śrī Balarāma, respectively, in the Kali-yuga.

GAUḌĪYA VAIṢṆAVA
a devotee of Śrī Kṛṣṇa, following in the footsteps of Śrī Caitanya Mahāprabhu.

GAUḌĪYA VAIṢṆAVISM
the practice of devotion to Viṣṇu/Kṛṣṇa according to the tenets of Śrī Caitanya Mahāprabhu.

GĪTĀ
see Bhagavad-gītā.

GĪTOPĀNIṢAD
another name for the Bhagavad-gītā, referring to its nature as an upaniṣad.

GOPĀLA
one of the holy names of Śrī Kṛṣṇa, referring to His childhood pastimes tending the calves in Vraja-maṇḍala.

GOPĪS
spiritual milkmaids of Vraja-maṇḍala who, of all devotees, exhibit the most intense love for Śrī Kṛṣṇa.

GOSVĀM
"master of the senses"; title of one who has accepted the renounced order of life.

GUṆAS
see Tri-guṇa.

GURU
a spiritual master; one who is heavy with knowledge of the Absolute and who removes nescience with the light of divine knowledge.

GURUDEVA/GURU MAHĀRĀJA
term of respect used to refer to one's spiritual master.

GURUVARGA
line of disciplic succession; the chain of gurus from past to present.

H

Hari

one of the holy names of the Supreme Lord, referring to His stealing the hearts of His devotees and taking away obstacles to their devotion.

Hari-Bhakti-Vilāsa

Vaiṣṇava smṛti, written by Śrīla Sanātana Gosvāmī and Śrīla Gopāla Bhaṭṭa dāsa Gosvāmī, elucidating the rules of Vaiṣṇava behavior.

Haridāsa Ṭhākura

expansion of Lord Brahmā in Caitanya-līlā. He is known as "Nāmācārya" or "the master of chanting the Holy Name" due to his chanting 300,000 names of the Lord daily.

Hari-kathā

discussion of the Name, Form, Attributes and Pastimes of the Supreme Lord.

Harināma

(1) the holy names of the Supreme Lord; (2) the practice of chanting the names of the Supreme Lord.

Hari-vāsara

Ekādaśī, which is very dear to the Supreme Lord.

Havana

Vedic fire sacrifice.

Hiraṇyakaśipu

the demon father of Prahlāda Mahārāja.

Hṛṣīkeśa

one of the holy names of the Supreme Lord, referring to Him as "Lord of the senses".

I

Indra

the king of the demigods. Also called Devarāja.

Indriyas

the gross and subtle senses.

J

Jagannātha

one of the holy names of Śrī Kṛṣṇa, referring to His pastime as "Lord of the Universe". In His deity form, He performs His processional pastime in the annual Ratha-yātrā festival in Purī and other places around the world.

Janmāṣṭamī

the holy appearance day of Śrī Kṛṣṇa.

JĪVĀ/JĪVĀTMĀ
(1) the individual soul; (2) the individual living entity.

JÑĀNA
knowledge.

JÑĀNĪ
one who follows the path of jñāna.

K

KALI-YUGA
the present era; the fourth of the four eras (catur-yuga) lasting 432,000 years. The lifespan of a human being during Kali-yuga is 100 years. The yuga-dharma of the Kali-yuga is chanting the Holy Name. Only one of the four kinds of piety (satyam, or truthfulness) is present during this era, in the form of the Holy Name itself.

KALPA
see catur-yuga.

KAPILADEVA
expansion of Kṛṣṇa; not to be confused with the atheistic philosopher, Kapila. The son of Devahūti and Kardama Muni. His life and teachings appear in the 3rd Canto of Śrīmad Bhāgavatam.

KĀMA
lust; the fulfillment of sensual desires.

KĀMYA-VANA
forest within Vraja-maṇḍala in which the Pāṇḍavas spent part of their twelve-year exile. It was there that Jayadhrata, the King of Sindhu, abducted Draupadī.

KANHAIYĀ
one of the names of Śrī Kṛṣṇa used with affection by the Vrajavāsis when Kṛṣṇa played the pastimes of a small boy.

KARMA
(1) work performed with self-interest in mind, as opposed to work performed in the interest of the Supreme Lord; (2) the laws of cause and effect within the material universe. See also Karma-kāṇḍa and karma-yoga.

KARMĪ
one who follows the path of karma (see also Karma-kāṇḍa).

KARMA-KĀṆḌA
section of the Vedic literatures that prescribes methods for the obtainment of temporary, material benefits.

KARMA-YOGA
the path of performing Karma.

KAṬHOPANIṢAD
one of the foremost of the eleven principal Upaniṣads. It relates the instructions of Yamarāja to the brāhmaṇa boy, Naciketā.

KAURAVAS
(1) the family of the Kuru dynasty; (2) the sons of Dhṛtarāṣṭra.

KAVIRĀJA GOSVĀMĪ
see Kṛṣṇadāsa Kavirāja.

KĪRTANA (OR SAṄKĪRTANA)
(1) chanting the glories of the Holy Name, form, pastimes of the Lord; (2) the practice of congregational chanting of the Holy Name to the accompaniment of drums, cymbals, etc.

KṚṢṆA
the original Holy Name of the Supreme Lord, referring to His unique position as the Ultimate Attractive Person. It also refers to His charming complexion, which resembles the hue of a monsoon cloud.

KṚṢṆADĀSA KAVIRĀJA
author of the sublime holy biography of Caitanya Mahāprabhu entitled "Caitanya Caritāmṛta".

KṚṢṆA-LĪLĀ
the pastimes of Śrī Kṛṣṇa in Vraja-maṇḍala.

KṚṢṆA-NĀMA
the holy names of Śrī Kṛṣṇa.

KṚṢṆA-PREMA
pure love for Supreme Lord Śrī Kṛṣṇa.

KṢATRIYA
the administrative/warrior class; their function is to govern and protect society according to the Vedic principles. One of the varṇas of the varṇāśrama system.

KUNTĪ DEVĪ
the wife of Pāṇḍu and one of the mothers of the Pāṇḍavas.

KURUKṢETRA
a sacred place of pilgrimage where, in ancient times, people traditionally went to bathe during a solar eclipse. It was here that the battle between the Kauravas and the Pāṇḍavas took place.

KURUS
see Kauravas.

L

LAKH
one hundred thousand.

LĪLĀ
transcendental, blissful activities or pastimes of the Supreme Lord and His pure devotees. See also Kṛṣṇa-līlā and Caitanya-līlā.

M

MAHĀBHĀRATA
epic literature of ancient India that narrates the story of a great battle, and the events leading up to it, that took place 5000 years ago. The principal figures in this story are Śrī Kṛṣṇa, the Pāṇḍavas and the Kauravas. The Bhagavad-gītā is one part of the Mahābhārata.

MAHĀDEVA
one of the names of Lord Śiva, meaning "the great demigod".

MAHĀJANA
"great soul" or "great person"; (1) a realized saint; (2) one of the twelve Mahājanas mentioned in Śrīmad Bhāgavatam; (3) a "money lender" (colloquial).

MAHĀMANTRA
"the great mantra" for deliverance: "Hare Kṛṣṇa, Hare Kṛṣṇa, Kṛṣṇa Kṛṣṇa, Hare Hare, Hare Rāma, Hare Rāma, Rāma Rāma, Hare Hare."

MAHĀPRABHU
honorific title meaning, "great master". A title reserved for Śrī Caitanya Mahāprabhu.

MAHĀRĀJA
"great king"; title given to a king, a sannyāsī or other elevated personalities.

MANTRA
combination of divine syllables, meditating upon which, one gets deliverance.

MANTRA-DĪKṢĀ
see dīkṣā.

MANU
a progenitor of mankind.

MAṬHA
monastery where students of the science of self-realization reside.

MĀRKEṆḌEYA ṚṢI
great sage who had been granted a lifespan of seven days of Brahmā (30,058,560,000 years) and to whom the Lord displayed His māyā potency. His biography is narrated in the 12th Canto of Śrīmad Bhāgavatam.

MṚKAṆḌA
the father of Mārkeṇḍeya Ṛṣi

MĀYĀ
the illusory potency of the Supreme Lord.

Māyāpura
: the holy birthplace of Śrī Caitanya Mahāprabhu, situated at the heart of Śrī Antardvīpa, one of the islands of Navadvīpa-dhāma, in West Bengal, India.

Mokṣa
: deliverance from the cycle of births and deaths.

Mukti
: see mokṣa

Mūrti
: (1) form (2) a temple deity.

N

Nakula
: the fourth of the five Pāṇḍava brothers.

Nāma-abhāsa
: a dim reflection or faint impression of the Holy Name. Example: Ajāmila called out the Holy Name of "Nārāyaṇa" when he was actually referring to his son.

Nāma-saṅkīrtana
: congregational chanting of the holy names of Śrī Kṛṣṇa.

Nanda Mahārāja
: One of Kṛṣṇa's fathers in Kṛṣṇa-līlā. His other father is Vasudeva.

Nandanandana
: one of the holy names of Śrī Kṛṣṇa, referring to his relationship as the son of Nanda Mahārāja.

Nārada Muni
: great devotee sage, who travels the length and breadth of both the spiritual and material worlds, singing and chanting the glories of Supreme Lord Śrī Kṛṣṇa, while playing his vina. One of the sons of Brahmā and one of the twelve Mahājanas.

Nārāyaṇa
: Kṛṣṇa, in His form of Viṣṇu, lying on the Causal Ocean; His majestic aspect as the Lord of Vaikuṇṭha. See also Viṣṇu.

Navadvīpa-dhāma
: Nine islands in West Bengal, India forming an eight-petalled lotus with Śrī Māyāpura (the holy birthplace of Śrī Caitanya Mahāprabhu) situated at its center.

Nityānanda Prabhu
: incarnation of Lord Balarāma in Caitanya-līlā; the guru of the universe and the intermediary between Śrī Caitanya Mahāprabhu and His devotees. See also Pañcatattva.

Nṛsiṁha/Nṛsiṁhadeva
: half-man/half-lion incarnation of Kṛṣṇa who is famous for rescuing His pure devotee, Prahlāda Mahārāja, from the demon Hiraṇyakaśipu. This story is narrated in the 7th Canto of Śrīmad Bhāgavatam.

NYĀYA
(1) justice; (2) the doctrines of logic.

P

PADMA PURĀṆA
one of the sāttvika Purāṇas, extolling the glories of Śrī Kṛṣṇa/Viṣṇu. So titled because it explains the creation of the world from the lotus stemming from the naval of Lord Viṣṇu. Also, the *padmā* (lotus) is described as the heart of Viṣṇu.

PAÑCATATTVA
God in five aspects, namely, Caitanya Mahāprabhu, Nityānanda Prabhu, Advaita Prabhu, Gadādhara Prabhu and Śrīvāsa Prabhu.

PĀṆḌAVAS
the five sons of Mahārāja Pāṇḍu, namely Yudhiṣṭhira, Bhīma, Arjuna, Sahadeva and Nakula.

PARAMĀTMĀ
expansion of Viṣṇu; the Supersoul or Oversoul; the indwelling monitor who guides the intelligence of the embodied living beings.

PĀRAṆA
the time of breaking a fast or vow.

PARĀ POTENCY
the superior or transcendental, spiritual potency of the Supreme Lord. See also Antaraṅgā-śakti.

PARAMGURUDEVA
the guru of one's guru.

PARIKRAMA
circumambulation of a holy site or deity.

PARĪKṢIT MAHĀRĀJA
the son of Abhimanyu and Uttarā. When the Pāṇḍavas retired from kingly life, he was crowned king of the entire world. He was cursed to die within seven days by the son of a brāhmaṇa. Renouncing everything, He spent these final days hearing the complete Śrī-mad Bhāgavatam from the lips of the great sage Śukadeva Gosvāmī.

PRABHU
honorific title meaning, "master".

PRAHLĀDA
great boy saint of ancient India who was rescued from the torment of his father, the demon Hiraṇyakaśipu, by the Supreme Lord in his form of Nṛsiṁhadeva.

PRĀṆAYĀMA
regulation of the breath in the practice of yoga.

PRASĀDA/PRASĀDAM
"mercy". Anything appropriate that has been offered to Supreme Lord Śrī Kṛṣṇa and, therefore, has become sanctified.

PREMA
pure, unconditional love; see Kṛṣṇa-prema.

PREMA-BHAKTI
pure, loving devotion.

PREYAḤ
immediate gratification of the senses.

PURĀṆAS
"primeval or ancient". Eighteen sacred Sanskrit literatures, divided into three categories (sāttvika, rājasika and tāmasika), which explain the Vedic philosophy by means of historical narratives.

PURUṢĀVATĀRA
the various Viṣṇu expansions of Kṛṣṇa, involved in the process of creation.

PURUṢOTTAMA-DHĀMA
City of Purī, Orissa, in India, in which the famous Jagannātha Temple is located. It is also the holy birthplace of Śrīla Bhaktisiddhānta Sarasvatī Ṭhākura.

R

RĀDHĀRĀṆĪ
the most beloved consort of Śrī Kṛṣṇa and the personification of the pleasure potency of Supreme Lord. She epitomizes the highest love for Sri Krsna.

RĀGA-BHAKTI
spontaneous devotion to Supreme Lord Śrī Kṛṣṇa.

RĀJASIKA
having the attributes of the mode of passion (Rajo-guṇa).

RAJO-GUṆA
the material quality, or mode, of passion.

RĀMACANDRA
incarnation of Śrī Kṛṣṇa. He is the great hero of the epic Rāmāyana, who defeated the demon, Rāvaṇa, who had abducted His wife, Sītā devī. He exemplifies the codes of dharma.

RĀMĀYANA
epic tale of the pastimes of Lord Rāmacandra, written by Śrī Vālmīki Muni.

RASA
the transcendental taste, or aesthetic, relished in the intimate relationships between Kṛṣṇa and His devotees.

RATHA-YĀTRĀ
annual chariot procession of Lord Jagannātha.

ṚṢABHADEVA
expansion of Śrī Kṛṣṇa. He is the father of Bharata Mahārāja and the Navayogendras. His life and teachings are narrated in the 5th Canto of Śrīmad Bhāgavatam.

ṚṢI
a sage.

RŪPA GOSVĀMĪ
chief of the six Gosvāmīs (intimate associates of Śrī Caitanya Mahāprabhu) known as "Rāsācārya" or "the great teacher of the subject of rasa". Founder of the Rādhā-Govindaji Temple in Vṛndāvana and author of Bhakti-Rasāmṛta-Sindhu, *Vidagdha Mādhava, Śrī Upadeśāmṛta* and many other superlative devotional literatures.

S

SACCIDĀNANDA
the principles of eternal existence (sat), knowledge/cognizance (cit) and bliss (ānanda).

SAD-GURU
a bonafide spiritual master.

SĀDHU
a pure devotee of Śrī Kṛṣṇa; one who has taken absolute shelter of the Lord.

SĀDHU-SAṄGA
keeping the company of sādhus.

SAHADEVA
the fifth and youngest of the five Pāṇḍava brothers. He was the son of Mādrī.

SAMA
being equal and impartial to all; one of the qualities of a sādhu.

SAMA-DARŚANA
equality of vision toward all living entities.

SANĀTANA-DHARMA
the eternal, intrinsic function of the individual living entity, i.e., devotional service to the Supreme Lord. Also called Bhāgavata-dharma.

SANĀTANĪ
a follower of sanātana-dharma.

SANDHYĀ
ablutions performed at the three junctions of the day (dawn, midday and dusk).

SAÑJAYA
minister who obtained a boon from Vyāsadeva Muni, allowing him a mystical vision of the events unfolding at the site of the battle of Kurukṣetra, so as to narrate the same to Dhṛtarāṣṭra.

Saṅkarācārya
expansion of Lord Śiva. Fulfilling the desire of Lord Viṣṇu, he promulgated the philosophy of undifferentiated monism in order to reinstate the authority of the Vedas, which had been negated by Buddhism.

Saṅkīrtana
congregational chanting of the Holy Name; see also kīrtana.

Saptārṣi
the seven ṛṣis of the Vedas. They are sons of Lord Brahmā.

Śāstra
"that which regulates"; sacred, divine scripture.

Sat
eternal existence; see also Saccidānanda

Sattva-guṇa
the material quality, or mode, of goodness.

Sāttvika
having the attributes of the mode of goodness (Sattva-guṇa).

Satya-loka
the planet of Lord Brahmā.

Satyam
truthfulness; one of the four kinds of piety: tapaḥ, śaucam, dayā and satyam (austerity, cleanliness, mercy and truthfulness). The only kind of piety remaining in the Kali-yuga, in the form of the Holy Name.

Satya-yuga
the first of the four eras (catur-yuga) lasting 1,728,000 years. The lifespan of a human being during Satya-yuga was 100,000 years. The dharma of the Satya-yuga was meditation. All four kinds of piety (tapaḥ, śaucam, dayā and satyam or austerity, cleanliness, mercy and truthfulness) were present during this era.

Śikṣā guru
instructing spiritual master.

Sītā Devī
wife of Lord Rāmacandra.

Śiva
great Vaiṣṇava demigod who is the controller of tamo-guṇa. Also called Mahādeva.

Śloka
a form of Sanskrit verse, originally composed by the author of the Rāmāyana, Śrī Vālmīki Muni.

Smaraṇaṁ
remembrance of the Holy Name, Form, Attributes and Pastimes of Supreme Lord.

SMĀRTA-BRĀHMAṆAS
(1) those brāhmaṇas who are well versed in smṛti; (2) proponents of the karma-kāṇḍa section of the Vedas.

SMṚTI
"that which is remembered"; (1) literatures supplementary to the Vedas and Upaniṣads, such as the Mahābhārata, Rāmāyaṇa and the Purāṇas. (2) smṛti-grantha.

SMṚTI-GRANTHA
literatures that delineate religious codes of behavior.

ŚRAVAṆAṀ
hearing about the Holy Name, Form, Attributes and Pastimes of the Supreme Lord.

ŚREYAḤ
one's ultimate good.

ŚRĪ/ŚRĪLA/ŚRĪMAD/ ŚRĪPĀDA
appellations of respect for great personalities.

ŚRĪNĀTHA CAKRAVARTĪ
great Vaiṣṇava saint who wrote Caitanya-manjusa, a commentary on Śrīmad Bhāgavatam.

ŚRĪMAD-BHĀGAVATAM
sublime, pure devotional literature describing, among other things, the creation of the world, the incarnations of Śrī Kṛṣṇa and the wonderful pastimes of Kṛṣṇa and His intimate devotees. The distilled essence of all Vedic knowledge. Also known as Bhāgavata Purāṇa.

ŚRĪVĀSA ṬHĀKURA
Incarnation of Nārada Muni in Caitanya-līlā. Among other things, he is renowned for the all-night kīrtanas held in the courtyard of his home. See also Pañcatattva.

ŚRUTI/ŚRUTI ŚĀSTRA
"that which is heard"; refers to the Vedas and Upaniṣads.

SUDARŚANA-CAKRA
the divine disc of Lord Viṣṇu.

ŚUDDHA BHAKTA
a pure devotee of Supreme Lord Śrī Kṛṣṇa

ŚUDDHA BHAKTI
pure devotion to Supreme Lord Śrī Kṛṣṇa.

ŚŪDRA
the laborer class, including artisans and craftsmen. One of the varṇas of the varṇāśrama system.

ŚUKADEVA GOSVĀMĪ
the great devotee sage who narrated Śrīmad Bhāgavatam to Mahārāja Parīkṣit.

Śvetadvīpa
the residence of Lord Viṣṇu in the material universe.

T

Tāmasika
having the attributes of the mode of ignorance (Tamo-guṇa).

Tamo-guṇa
the material quality, or mode, of ignorance.

Taṭasthā-śakti
the marginal energy of the Supreme Lord; the jīvātmās, or individual living beings, are situated at the *taṭa*, or boundary line, between the internal and the external potencies and have the tendency to go toward either the spiritual realm or the material world.

Tapaḥ
austerity; one of the four kinds of piety: tapaḥ, śaucam, dayā, and satyam (austerity, cleanliness, mercy and truthfulness).

Tithi
a day of the lunar month.

Tretā-yuga
the second of the four eras (catur-yuga) lasting 1,296,000 years. The lifespan of a human being during Tretā-yuga was 10,000 years. The yuga-dharma of the Tretā-yuga was sacrifice. Three of the four kinds of piety (śaucam, dayā and satyam or cleanliness, mercy and truthfulness) were present during this era.

Tridaṇḍi
one who carries a triple staff, indicating complete dedication of body, mind and words to Supreme Lord Śrī Kṛṣṇa, i.e., a Vaiṣṇava sannyāsī.

Tri-guṇa
the three primal material qualities or "modes". See also sattva-guṇa, rajo-guṇa and tamo-guṇa.

Tulāsī Devī
see Vṛndā Devī.

U

Uddhava
disciple of Bṛhaspati and intimate associate of Lord Kṛṣṇa in Dvārakā.

Upādhi
a mundane designation.

Upaniṣad
philosophical portion of the Vedas that must be learned at the foot of a spiritual master. There are 108 Upaniṣads, eleven of which are principal.

V

VAIDHĪ-BHAKTI
bhakti performed as per the injunctions of the scriptures.

VAIKUṆṬHA
realm of the spiritual planets, where there is no anxiety.

VAIṢṆAVA
a pure devotee of Śrī Viṣṇu/Kṛṣṇa.

VAIṢṆAVISM
pure devotion to Śrī Viṣṇu/Kṛṣṇa; the eternal and natural function of the living being.

VAIŚYA
the mercantile/agricultural class; their function is to maintain the economic affairs of society according to the Vedic principles; one of the varṇas of the varṇāśrama system.

VAṀSĪ DĀSA BĀBĀJĪ MAHĀRĀJA
great renunciate devotee who entered the eternal līlā of Sri Krsna in 1944.

VANA
a forest.

VANACĀRĪ
a person in the retired order of life.

VANA-PARVA
section of the Mahābhārata that narrates the twelve-year exile of the Pāṇḍavas in the forest.

VARṆA
any of the four social classes within the varṇāśrama system (namely, brāhmaṇa, kṣatriya, Vaiśya and śūdra).

VARṆĀŚRAMA SYSTEM
Vedic social system consisting of four major categories of varṇa or social class (namely, brāhmaṇa, kṣatriya, Vaiśya and śūdra) and four categories of āśramas or orders of life (namely, brahmacārī, gṛhastha, vanacārī and sannyāsī).

VASUDEVA
One of Kṛṣṇa's fathers in Kṛṣṇa-līlā. His other father is Nanda Mahārāja.

VĀSUDEVA
one of the holy names of Śrī Kṛṣṇa, defining His relationship as the son of Vasudeva and also referring to Him as the "One Who Dwells Everywhere".

VEDAS
"books of knowledge"; the sacred scriptures of ancient India covering all branches of knowledge.

VEDIC
referring to the Vedas or things connected with them.

VEDAVYĀSA MUNI
: an expansion of Kṛṣṇa. He is the compiler of the Vedic literatures.

VIṢAYA
: an object of enjoyment.

VIŚVANĀTHA CAKRAVARTĪ
: great Vaiṣṇava saint noted for his commentaries on Śrīmad Bhāgavatam and Bhagavad-gītā. He is the author of numerous beautiful devotional songs, and literatures such as *Śrī Kṛṣṇa-bhāvanāmṛta, Mādhurya-kādambinī* and many others.

VIṢṆU
: one of the holy names of Śrī Kṛṣṇa, referring to His all-pervasiveness. Also called Nārāyaṇa.

VRAJA-DHĀMA/VRAJA-MAṆḌALA
: the holy site of Kṛṣṇa's pastimes on earth, non-different from His abode in Vaikuṇṭha. It consists of twelve sacred forests, Vṛndāvana being one of them.

VRAJAVĀSIS
: the holy residents of Vraja-dhāma.

VṚNDĀ DEVĪ
: expansion of Rādhārāṇī who adopted the form of the sacred Tulāsī plant and also the Gaṇḍakī River.

VṚNDĀVANA
: that place where the Name, Fame, Qualities and Paraphernalia of Supreme Lord Kṛṣṇa are always present; the transcendental dwelling place of Śrī Kṛṣṇa in the spiritual world where the mood of sweetness prevails, which is identical with the town of Vṛndāvana in Northwest India, where Kṛṣṇa performed His pastimes 5000 years ago. Vṛndāvana means "the forest where Śrīmatī Vṛndā Devī grows". See also Vraja-dhāma.

VṚNDĀVANA DĀSA ṬHĀKURA
: 16th century author of the Caitanya Bhāgavata, a sacred literature narrating the holy life and pastimes of Śrī Caitanya Mahāprabhu.

VṚNDĀVANA-DHĀMA
: refers to the general area of Vṛndāvana.

VYĀSADEVA MUNI
: see Vedavyāsa Muni

Y

YAJÑA
: sacrifice or the performance of a sacrifice. Also a Name for Kṛṣṇa.

YAMADŪTAS
: the messengers of the god of death.

YĀMA-PURĪ
: the realm of the god of death.